Beginning Ethereum Smart Contracts Programming

With Examples in Python, Solidity, and JavaScript

Wei-Meng Lee

Apress®

Beginning Ethereum Smart Contracts Programming: With Examples in Python,
Solidity, and JavaScript

Wei-Meng Lee
Ang Mo Kio, Singapore

ISBN-13 (pbk): 978-1-4842-5085-3   ISBN-13 (electronic): 978-1-4842-5086-0
https://doi.org/10.1007/978-1-4842-5086-0

Managing Director, Apress Media LLC: Welmoed Spahr
Acquisitions Editor: Joan Murray
Development Editor: Laura Berendson
Coordinating Editor: Jill Balzano

Cover image Photo by Bryan Garces on Unsplash

Distributed to the book trade worldwide by Springer Science+Business Media New York, 233 Spring Street, 6th Floor, New York, NY 10013. Phone 1-800-SPRINGER, fax (201) 348-4505, e-mail orders-ny@springer-sbm.com, or visit www.springeronline.com. Apress Media, LLC is a California LLC and the sole member (owner) is Springer Science + Business Media Finance Inc (SSBM Finance Inc). SSBM Finance Inc is a **Delaware** corporation.

For information on translations, please e-mail rights@apress.com, or visit http://www.apress.com/rights-permissions.

Apress titles may be purchased in bulk for academic, corporate, or promotional use. eBook versions and licenses are also available for most titles. For more information, reference our Print and eBook Bulk Sales web page at http://www.apress.com/bulk-sales.

Any source code or other supplementary material referenced by the author in this book is available to readers on GitHub via the book's product page, located at www.apress.com/9781484250853. For more detailed information, please visit http://www.apress.com/source-code.

Printed on acid-free paper

I dedicate this book with love to my dearest wife (Sze Wa)
and daughter (Chloe), who have to endure
my irregular work schedule, for their companionship
when I am trying to meet writing deadlines!

Table of Contents

About the Author

 **Wei-Meng Lee** is the founder of Developer Learning Solutions, a technology company specializing in hands-on training of blockchain and other emerging technologies. He has many years of training expertise, and his courses emphasize a learn-by-doing approach. He is a master at making learning a new programming language or technology less intimidating and fun. He can be found speaking at conferences worldwide such as NDC, and he regularly contributes to online and print publications such as DevX.com, MobiForge.com, and CoDe Magazine. He is active on social media on his blog learn2develop.net, on Facebook at DeveloperLearningSolutions, on Twitter @weimenglee, and on LinkedIn at leeweimeng.

About the Technical Reviewer

 **Chaim Krause** is a lover of computers, electronics, animals, and electronic music. He's tickled pink when he can combine two or more in some project. The vast majority of his knowledge is through self-learning. He jokes with everyone that the only difference between what he does at home and what he does at work is the logon he uses. As a lifelong learner, he is often frustrated with technical errors in documentation that waste valuable time and cause unnecessary stress. One of the reasons he works as the technical editor on books is to help others avoid those same pitfalls.

Acknowledgments

Writing a book is immensely exciting, but along with it comes long hours of hard work and responsibility, straining to get things done accurately and correctly. To make a book possible, a lot of unsung heroes work tirelessly behind the scenes.

For this, I would like to take this opportunity to thank a number of special people who made this book possible. First, I want to thank my acquisitions editor – Joan Murray, for giving me this opportunity. Thanks for attending my session at NDC Minnesota 2018, and for your trust in me!

Next, a huge thanks to Jill Balzano, my associate editor, who was always very patient with me, even though I have missed several of my deadlines for the book. Thanks, Jill, for your guidance. I could not finish the book without your encouragement and help!

Equally important is my technical editor – Chaim Krause. Chaim has been very eager-eyed editing and testing my code and never fails to let me know if things do not work the way I intended. Thanks for catching my errors and making the book a better read, Chaim!

Last, but not least, I want to thank my parents and my wife, Sze Wa, for all the support they have given me. They have selflessly adjusted their schedules to accommodate my busy schedule when I was working on this book. I love you all!

Introduction

Welcome to *Beginning Ethereum Smart Contracts Programming*!

This book is a quick guide to getting started with Ethereum Smart Contracts programming. It first starts off with a discussion on blockchain and the motivations behind it. You will learn what is a blockchain, how blocks in a blockchain are chained together, and how blocks get added to a blockchain. You will also understand how mining works and discover the various types of nodes in a blockchain network.

Once that is out of the way, we will dive into the Ethereum blockchain. You will learn how to use an Ethereum client (Geth) to connect to the Ethereum blockchain and perform transactions such as sending ethers to another account. You will also learn how to create private blockchain networks so that you can test them internally within your own network.

The next part of this book will discuss Smart Contracts programming, a unique feature of the Ethereum blockchain. Readers will be able to get jumpstarted on Smart Contracts programming without needing to wade through tons of documentation. The learn-by-doing approach of this book makes you productive in the shortest amount of time. By the end of this book, you would be able to write smart contracts, test them, deploy them, and create web applications to interact with them.

The last part of this book will touch on tokens, something that has taken the cryptocurrency market by storm. You would be able to create your own tokens and launch your own ICO and would be able to write token contracts that allow buyers to buy tokens using Ethers.

This book is for those who want to get started quickly with Ethereum Smart Contracts programming. Basic programming knowledge and an understanding of Python or JavaScript are recommended.

I hope you will enjoy working on the sample projects as much as I have enjoyed working on them!

CHAPTER 1

Understanding Blockchain

One of the hottest technologies of late is *Blockchain*. But what exactly is a blockchain? And how does it actually work? In this chapter, we will explore the concept of blockchain, how the concept was conceived, and what problems it aimed to solve. By the end of this chapter, the idea and motivation behind blockchain would be crystal clear.

Tip For the clearly impatient – A blockchain is a digital transaction of records that's arranged in chunks of data called blocks. These blocks link with one another through a cryptographic validation known as a hashing function. Linked together, these blocks form an unbroken chain – a blockchain. A blockchain is programmed to record not only financial transactions but virtually everything of value. Another name for blockchain is *distributed ledger*.

Hold on tight, as I'm going to discuss a lot of concepts in this chapter. But if you follow along closely, you'll understand the concepts of blockchain and be on your way to creating some really creative applications on the Ethereum blockchain in the upcoming chapters!

Tip Ethereum is an open-source public blockchain that is similar to the Bitcoin network. Besides offering a cryptocurrency known as Ether (which is similar to Bitcoin), the main difference between Bitcoin and itself is that it offers a programming platform on top of the blockchain, called Smart Contract. This book focuses on the Ethereum blockchain and Smart Contract.

© Wei-Meng Lee 2019
W.-M. Lee, *Beginning Ethereum Smart Contracts Programming*,
https://doi.org/10.1007/978-1-4842-5086-0_1

Motivations Behind Blockchain

Most people have heard of cryptocurrencies, or at least, Bitcoin.

Note   The technology behind cryptocurrencies is blockchain.

To understand why we need cryptocurrencies, you have to first start with understanding a fundamental concept – *trust*. Today, any asset of value or transaction is recorded by a third party, such as bank, government, or company. We trust banks won't steal our money, and they are regulated by the government. And even If the banks fail, it is backed by the government. We also trust our credit card companies – sellers trust credit card companies to pay them the money, and buyers trust credit card companies to settle any disputes with the sellers.

Placement of Trusts

All these boil down to one key concept – placement of trust. And that is, we place our trust on a central body. Think about it, in our everyday life, we place our trusts on banks, and we place our trusts on our governments.

Even for simple mundane day-to-day activities, we place our trusts in central bodies. For example, when you go to the library to borrow a book, you trust that the library would maintain a proper record of the books that you have borrowed and returned.

The key theme is that we trust institutions but don't trust each other. We trust our government, banks, even our library, but we just don't trust each other. As an example, consider the following scenario. Imagine you work at a cafe, and someone walks up to you and offers you a US ten-dollar bill for two cups of coffee. And another person who offers to pay you for the two cups of coffee using a handwritten note saying he owes you ten dollars. Which one would you trust? The answer is pretty obvious, isn't it? Naturally you would trust the US ten-dollar bill, as opposed to the handwritten note. This is because you understand that using the ten-dollar bill, you can use it elsewhere to exchange for other goods or services, and that it is backed by the US government. In contract, the handwritten note is not backed by anyone else (except perhaps the person who wrote it), and hence it has literally no value.

Now let's take the discussion a bit further. Again, imagine you are trying to sell something. Someone comes up to you and suggests paying for your goods using the currencies as shown in Figure 1-1.

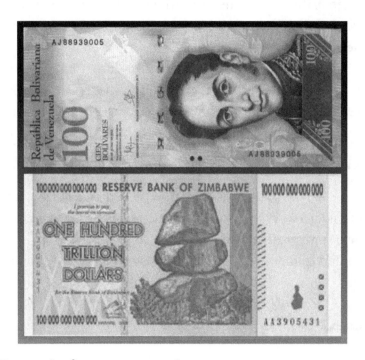

Figure 1-1. *Currencies from two countries*

Would you accept the currencies as shown in the figure? Here, you have two different currencies – one from Venezuela and one from Zimbabwe. In this case, the first thing you consider is whether these currencies are widely accepted and also your trust in these governments. You might have read from the news about the hyperinflation in these two countries, and that these currencies might not retain its value over time.

And so, would you accept these currencies as payment?

Trust Issues

Earlier on, I mentioned that people trust institutions and don't trust each other. But even established economies can fail, such as in the case of the financial crisis of the United States in 2007–2008. Investment bank Lehman Brothers collapsed in September 2008 because of the subprime mortgage market. So, if banks from established economies can collapse, how can people in less developed countries trust their banks and governments? Even if the banks are trusted, your deposits may be monitored by the government, and they could arrest you based on your transactions.

As we have seen in the example in the previous section, there are times when people don't trust institutions, especially if the political situation in that country is not stable.

All these discussions bring us to the next key issue – even though people trust institutions, institutions can still fail. And when people lose trust in institutions, people turn to *cryptocurrencies*. In the next section, we will discuss how we can solve the trust issues using *decentralization*, a fundamental concept behind cryptocurrency.

Solving Trust Issues Using Decentralization

Now that you have seen the challenges of trust – who to trust and who not to trust, it is now time to consider a way to solve the trust issues. In particular, blockchain uses decentralization to solve the trust issue.

In order to understand decentralization, let's use a very simple example that is based on our daily lives.

Example of Decentralization

To understand how decentralization solves the trust issue, let's consider a real-life example.

Imagine a situation where you have three persons with DVDs that they want to share with one another (see Figure 1-2).

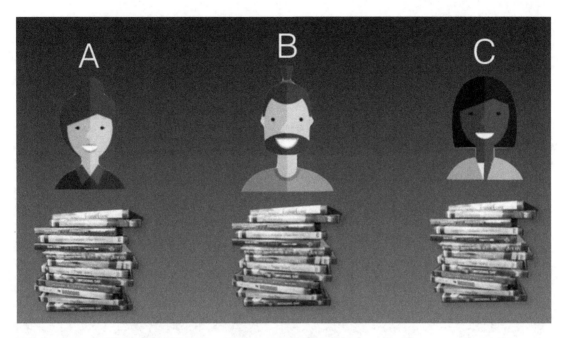

Figure 1-2. *Sharing DVDs among a group of people*

The first thing they need to do is to have someone keep track of the whereabouts of each DVD. Of course, the easiest is for each person to keep track of what they have borrowed and what they have lent, but since people inherently do not trust each other, this approach is not very popular among the three persons.

To solve this issue, they decided to appoint one person, say B, to keep a ledger, to hold a record of the whereabouts of each DVD (see Figure 1-3).

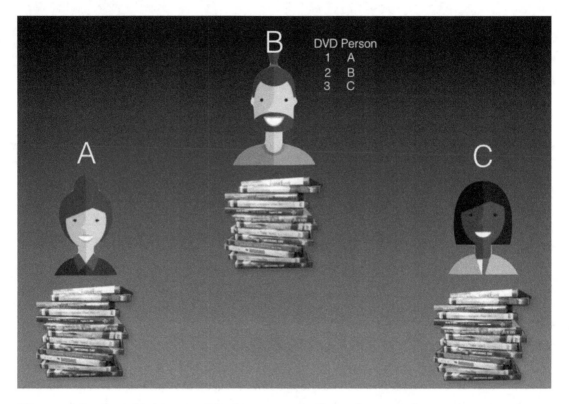

Figure 1-3. *Appointing a particular person to keep the records*

This way, there is a central body to keep track of the whereabouts of each DVD. But wait, isn't this the problem with centralization? What happens if B is not trustworthy? Turns out that B has the habit of stealing DVDs, and he in fact could easily modify the ledger to erase the record of DVDs that he has borrowed. So, there must be a better way.

And then, someone has an idea! Why not let everyone keep a copy of the ledger (see Figure 1-4)? Whenever someone borrows or lent a DVD, the record is broadcast to everyone, and everyone records the transaction.

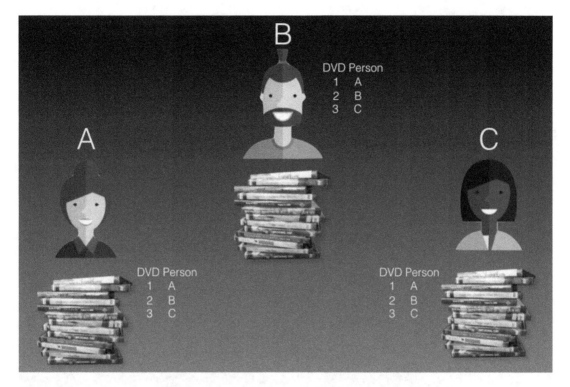

Figure 1-4. *Getting everyone to keep the records*

We say that the record keeping is now decentralized! We now have three persons holding the same ledger. But wait a minute. What if A and C conspire to change the records together so that they can steal the DVDs from B? Since majority wins, as long as there is more than 50% of the people with the same records, the others would have to listen to the majority. And because there are only three persons in this scenario, it is extremely easy to get more than 50% of the people to conspire.

The solution is to have a lot more people to hold the ledger, especially people who are not related to the DVDs sharing business (see Figure 1-5).

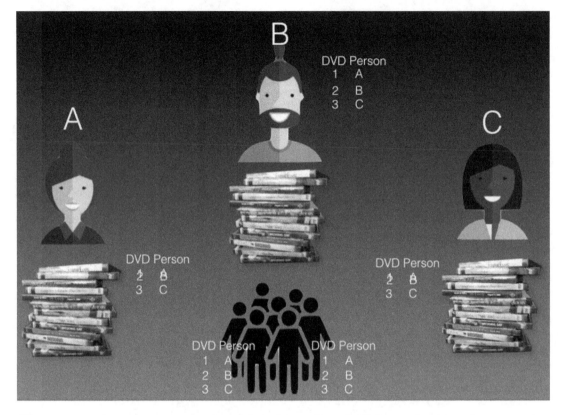

Figure 1-5. *Getting a group of unrelated people to help keep the records*

This way, it makes it more difficult for one party to alter the records on the ledger, and that in order to alter a record, it would need to involve a number of people altering the record all at the same time, which is a time-consuming affair. And this is the key idea behind *distributed ledger*, or commonly known as blockchain.

Blockchain As a Distributed Ledger

Now that we have a better idea of a distributed ledger, we can now associate it with the term – blockchain. Using the DVD rental example, each time a DVD is borrowed or returned, a transaction is created. A number of transactions are then grouped into a block. As more transactions are performed, the blocks are linked together cryptographically, forming what we now call a blockchain (see Figure 1-6).

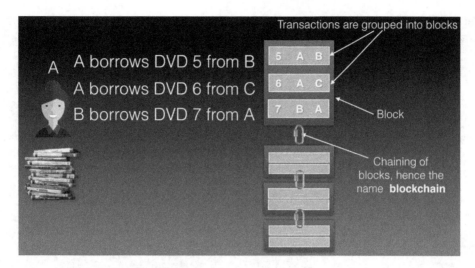

Figure 1-6. *Transactions form a block, and then blocks are then chained*

Based on what we have discussed, we can now summarize a few important points:

- Centralized databases and institutions work when there is trust in the system of law, governments, regulatory bodies, and people.

- A decentralized database built on the blockchain removes the need for the trust in a central body.

- A blockchain can be used for anything of value, not just currencies.

How Blockchain Works

At a very high level, a blockchain consists of a number of blocks. Each block contains a list of transactions, as well as a timestamp (see Figure 1-7).

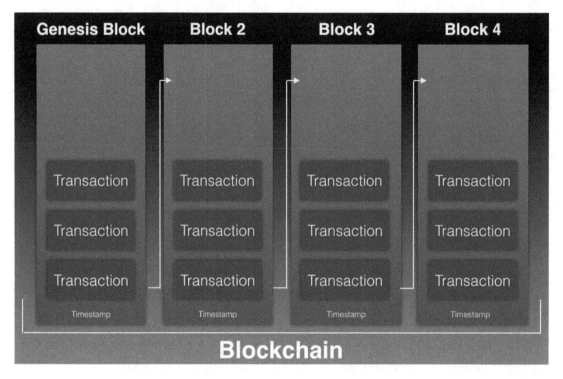

Figure 1-7. *Every blockchain has a beginning block known as the genesis block*

The blocks are connected to each other cryptographically, the details in which we will discuss in the sections ahead. The first block in a blockchain is known as the *genesis* block.

Note   Every blockchain has a genesis block.

So, the next important questions is – how do you chain the blocks together?

Chaining the Blocks

Before we discuss how blocks in a blockchain are chained together, we have to discuss a key concept in blockchain – hashing. A hash function is a function that maps data of arbitrary size to data of fixed size. By altering a single character in the original string, the resultant hash value is totally different from the previous one. Most importantly, observe that a single change in the original message results in a completely different hash, making it difficult to know that the two original messages are similar.

A hash function has the following characteristics:

- It is deterministic – the same message always results in the same hash.

- It is a one-way process – when you hash a string, it is computationally hard to reverse a hash to its original message.

- It is collision resistant – it is hard to find two different input messages that hash to the same hash.

We are now ready to discuss how blocks in a blockchain are chained together. To chain the blocks together, the content of each block is hashed and then stored in the next block (see Figure 1-8). That way, if any transactions in a block is altered, that is going to invalidate the hash of the current block, which is stored in the next block, which in turn is going to invalidate the hash of the next block, and so on.

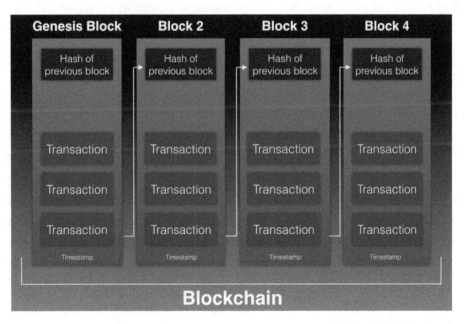

Figure 1-8. *Chaining the blocks with hashes*

Observe that when hashing the content of a block, the hash of the previous block is hashed together with the transactions. However, do take note that this is a simplification of what is in a block. Later on, we will dive into the details of a block and see exactly how transactions are represented in a block.

Storing the hash of the previous block in the current block assures the integrity of the transactions in the previous block. Any modifications to the transaction(s) within a block causes the hash in the next block to be invalidated, and it also affects the subsequent blocks in the blockchain. If a hacker wants to modify a transaction, not only must he modify the transaction in a block but all other subsequent blocks in the blockchain. In addition, he needs to synchronize the changes to all other computers on the network, which is a computationally expensive task to do. Hence, data stored in the blockchain is immutable, for they are hard to change once the block they are in is added to the blockchain.

Up to this point, you have a high-level overview of what constitutes a blockchain and how the blocks are chained together. In the next section, you will understand the next important topic in blockchain – mining.

Mining

Whenever you talk about blockchain or cryptocurrencies, there is always one term that comes up – mining. In this section, you will learn what is mining, and what goes on behind the scene.

Mining is the process of adding blocks to a blockchain. In a blockchain network, such as the Bitcoin or Ethereum network, there are different types of computers known as nodes. Computers on a blockchain that add blocks to the blockchain are known as *miner nodes* (or *mining nodes*, or more simply *miners*).

We will talk about the different types of nodes later on in this course, but for now, we want to talk about a particular type of node, known as the miner node. The role of the miner node is to add blocks to the blockchain.

But how are blocks added?

Broadcasting Transactions

When a transaction is performed, the transaction is broadcasted to the network (see Figure 1-9).

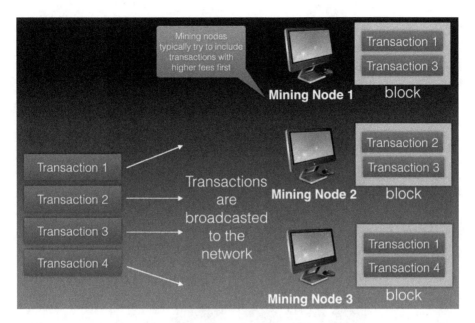

Figure 1-9. *Transactions are broadcasted to mining nodes, which then assemble them into blocks to be mined*

Each mining node may receive them at different times. As a node receives transactions, it will try to include them in a block. Observe that each node is free to include whatever transactions they want in a block. In practice, which transactions get included in a block depends on a number of factors, such as transaction fees, transaction size, order of arrival, and so on.

At this point, transactions that are included in a block but which are not yet added to the blockchain are known as *unconfirmed transactions*. Once a block is filled with transactions, a node will attempt to add the block to the blockchain.

Now here comes the problem – with so many miners out there, who gets to add the block to the blockchain first?

The Mining Process

In order to slow down the rate of adding blocks to the blockchain, the *blockchain consensus protocol* dictates a network difficulty target (see Figure 1-10).

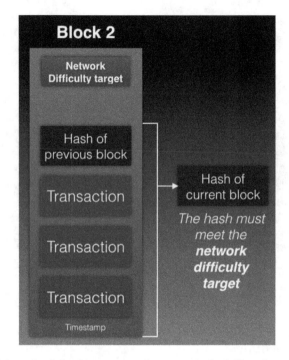

Figure 1-10. *Hashing the block to meet the network difficulty target*

In order to successfully add a block to the blockchain, a miner would hash the content of a block and check that the hash meets the criteria set by the difficulty target. For example, the resultant hash must start with five zeros and so on.

As more miners join the network, the difficultly level increases, for example, the hash must now start with six zeros and so on. This allows the blocks to be added to the blockchain at a consistent rate.

But, wait a minute, the content of a block is fixed, and so no matter how you hash it, the resultant hash is always the same. So how do you ensure that the resultant hash can meet the difficulty target? To do that, miners add a nonce to the block, which stands for *number used once* (see Figure 1-11).

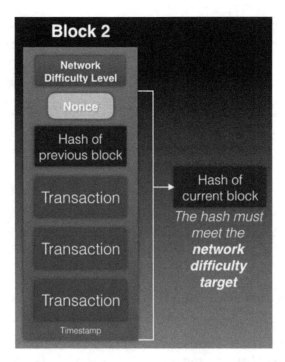

Figure 1-11. *Adding a nonce to change the content of the block in order to meet the network difficulty target*

The first miner who meets the target gets to claim the rewards and adds the block to the blockchain. It will broadcast the block to other nodes so that they can verify the claim and stop working on their current work of mining their own blocks. The miners would drop their current work, and the process of mining a new block starts all over again. The transactions that were not included in the block that was successfully mined will be added to the next block to be mined.

REWARDS FOR MINERS

In the case of Bitcoin, the block reward initially was 50 BTC and will halve every 210,000 blocks. At the time of writing, the block reward is currently at 12.5 BTC, and it will eventually be reduced to 0 after 64 halving events. For Ethereum, the reward for mining a block is currently 2 ETH (Ether).

BLOCKS ADDING RATES

For Bitcoin, the network adjusts the difficulty of the puzzles so that a new block is being mined roughly every 10 minutes. For Ethereum, a block is mined approximately every 14 seconds.

Proof of Work

The process in which blocks are mined and added to the blockchain is known as the **Proof of Work** (**PoW**). It is difficult to produce the proof but very easy to validate. A good example of Proof of Work is cracking a combination lock – it takes a lot of time to find the right combination, but it is easy to verify once the combination is found.

Proof of Work uses tremendous computing resources – GPUs are required, while CPU speed is not important. It also uses a lot of electricity, because miners are doing the same work repeatedly – find the nonce to meet the network difficulty for the block.

A common question is why you need to use a powerful GPU instead of CPU for mining? Well, as a simple comparison, a CPU core can execute 4 32-bit instructions per clock, whereas a GPU like the Radeon HD 5970 can execute 3200 32-bit instructions per clock. In short, the CPU excels at doing complex manipulations to a small set of data, whereas the GPU excels at doing simple manipulations to a large set of data. And since mining is all about performing hashing and finding the nonce, it is a highly repetitive task, something that GPU excels in.

Tip   When a miner has successfully mined a block, he earns mining fees as well as transaction fees. That's what keeps miners motivated to invest in mining rigs and keep them running 24/7, thereby incurring substantial electricity bills.

Immutability of Blockchains

In a blockchain, each block is chained to its previous block through the use of a cryptographic hash. A block's identity changes if the parent's identity changes. This in turn causes the current block's children to change, which affects the grandchildren, and so on. A change to a block forces a recalculation of all subsequent blocks, which requires enormous computation power. This makes the blockchain immutable, a key feature of cryptocurrencies like Bitcoin and Ethereum.

As a new block is added to the blockchain, the block of transactions is said to be *confirmed* by the blockchain. When a block is newly added, it's deemed to have one confirmation. As another block is added to it, its number of confirmation increases. Figure 1-12 shows the number of confirmations that the blocks in a blockchain have. The more confirmations a block has, the more difficult it is to remove it from the blockchain.

Tip   In general, once a block has six or more confirmations, it's deemed infeasible for it to be reversed. Therefore, the data stored in the blockchain is immutable.

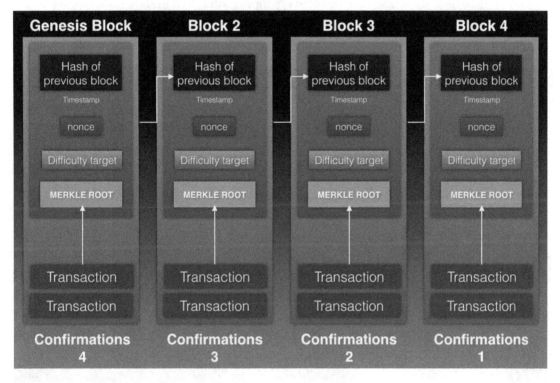

Figure 1-12. *Confirmations of blocks in a blockchain*

Blockchain in More Detail

In the previous section, you learned that a block contains a nonce, timestamp, and the list of transactions. That was a simplification. In real implementation, a block consists of

- A block header
- The list of transactions

The block header in turn consists of the following:

- The hash of the previous block

- Timestamp

- Merkle root

- Nonce

- Network difficulty target

Note that the block header contains the *Merkle root*, and not the transactions (see Figure 1-13). The transactions are collectively represented as a merkle root, details of which will be discussed in the next few sections.

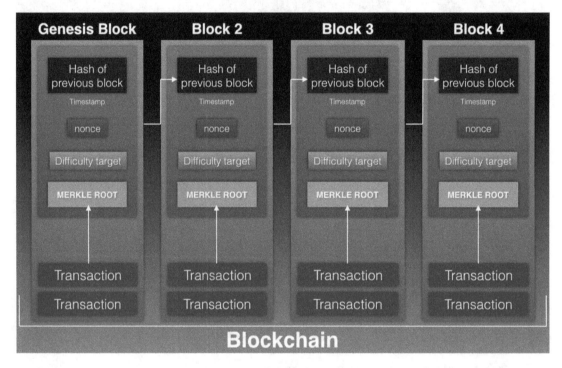

Figure 1-13. *A block contains the block header, which in turns contains the Merkle root of the transactions*

Types of Nodes

Before we address the rationale for storing the Merkle root in the block header, we need to talk about the types of nodes in a blockchain network. Figure 1-14 shows the different types of nodes in a blockchain network.

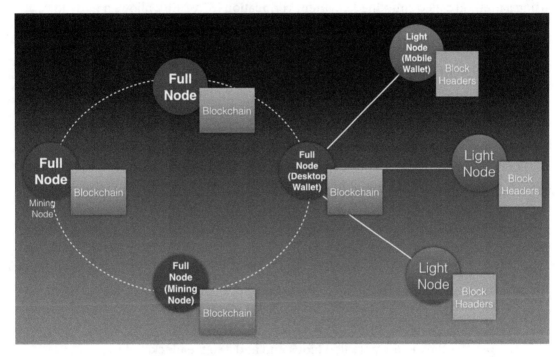

Figure 1-14. *Different types of nodes in a blockchain network*

As we mentioned in our earlier sections, computers connected to the blockchain network are known as nodes. We have discussed the role of mining nodes, whose key responsibility is to gather transactions into blocks and then try to add the block to the blockchain by finding the nonce that satisfies the network difficulty. Mining nodes are also known as *full nodes*.

Tip   Note that full nodes are not necessarily mining nodes. However, mining nodes need to be a full node.

The purpose of a full node is to ensure the integrity of the blockchain and people running full nodes do not get rewards. On the other hand, mining nodes are rewarded when they add a block to the blockchain.

An example of a full node is a desktop wallet, which allows users to perform transaction using the cryptocurrency.

Each full node has a copy of the entire blockchain. Full nodes also validate every block and transactions presented to it.

Besides full nodes, there are also *light nodes*. Light nodes help to verify transactions using a method called simplified payment verification (SPV). SPV allows a node to verify if a transaction has been included in a block, without needing to download the entire blockchain. Using SPV, light nodes connect to full nodes and transmit transactions to the full nodes for verifications.

Light nodes only need to store the block headers of all the blocks in the blockchain. An example of a light node is a mobile wallet, such as the Coinbase mobile app for iOS and Android. Using a mobile wallet, a user can perform transactions on the mobile device.

Note   Desktop wallets can be full node or light node.

And so, we can summarize the types of nodes that we have discussed thus far:

- Full node

  - Maintains a complete copy of the blockchain

  - Able to verify all transactions since the beginning

  - Verifies a newly created block and add it to the blockchain

  - Visit the following sites to see the current number of full nodes for the following blockchains:

    - Bitcoin – `https://bitnodes.earn.com`

    - Ethereum – `www.ethernodes.org/network/1`

- Mining node (must be a full node)

  - Works on a problem (finding the nonce)

- Light node (e.g., wallets)

  - Maintains the headers of the blockchain

  - Uses SPV to verify if a transaction is present and valid in a block

Finally, let's now see the use of representing the transactions as a Merkle root in the block header in the next section.

Merkle Tree and Merkle Root

The list of transactions in a block is stored as a *Merkle tree*. A Merkle tree is a tree data structure in which every leaf node is the hash of a transaction and every non-leaf node is the cryptographic hash of the child nodes. Figure 1-15 shows how the Merkle root is derived from the transactions.

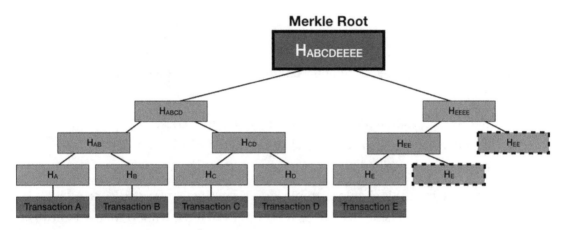

Figure 1-15. *How the Merkle root is derived from the Merkle tree*

As you can see from the figure, each transaction is hashed. The hash of each transaction is hashed together with the hash of another node. For example, the hash of transaction A (H_A) is combined with the hash of transaction B (H_B) and hashed to derive H_{AB}. This process is repeated until there's only one resultant hash. This final hash is known as the Merkle root. In the preceding example, because H_E doesn't have another node to pair with, it's hashed with itself. The same applies to H_{EE}.

The Merkle root is stored in the block header, and the rest of the transactions are stored in the block as a Merkle tree. In the earlier discussion, I mentioned about full nodes. Full nodes download the entire blockchain, and there's another type of node (known as *light nodes*) that downloads only the blockchain headers. Because light nodes don't download the entire blockchain, they're easier to maintain and run. Using a method called *simplified payment verifications* (SPV), a light node can query a full node to verify a transaction. Examples of light nodes are cryptographic wallets.

Uses of Merkle Tree and the Merkle Root

By storing the Merkle root in the block header and the transactions as a Merkle tree in the block, a light node can easily verify if a transaction belongs to a particular block. This is how it works. Suppose a light node wants to verify that transaction C exists in a particular block:

- The light node queries a full node for the following hashes: H_D, H_{AB}, and H_{EEEE} (see Figure 1-16).

- Because the light node can compute H_C, it can then compute H_{CD} with H_D supplied.

- With H_{AB} supplied, it can now compute H_{ABCD}.

- With H_{EEEE} supplied, it can now compute $H_{ABCDEEEE}$ (which is the Merkle root).

- Because the light node has the Merkle root of the block, it can now check to see if the two Merkle roots match. If they match, the transaction is verified.

As you can see from this simple example, to verify a single transaction out of five transactions, only three hashes need to be retrieved from the full node. Mathematically, for n transactions in a block, it takes $\log_2 n$ hashes to verify that a transaction is in a block. For example, if there are 1024 transactions in a block, a light node only needs to request ten hashes to verify the existence of a transaction in the block.

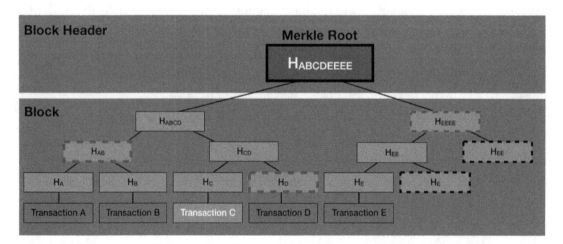

Figure 1-16. *How the Merkle tree and Merkle root are used to validate a transaction*

Summary

In this chapter, you have learned about the motivations behind blockchain and the problems that it aims to solve. You also had a chance to know how blocks are added to the blockchain through a process known as mining. In the next chapter, you will learn how to build your own blockchain using Python so that you can see and understand the inner workings of a blockchain.

CHAPTER 2

Implementing Your Own Blockchain Using Python

In the previous chapter, you learned about the basics of blockchain – the motivations behind blockchains, how transactions are added to blocks, and how blocks are added to the previous blocks to form a chain of blocks called blockchain. A good way to understand all these concepts would be to build one yourself. By implementing your own blockchain, you will have a more detailed look at how concepts like transactions, mining, and consensus work.

Obviously, implementing a full blockchain is not for the faint of heart, and that is definitely not our goal in this chapter. What we will try to do in this chapter is to implement a conceptual blockchain using Python and use it to illustrate the key concepts.

Our Conceptual Blockchain Implementation

For this chapter, we will build a very simple blockchain as shown in Figure 2-1.

© Wei-Meng Lee 2019
W.-M. Lee, *Beginning Ethereum Smart Contracts Programming*,
https://doi.org/10.1007/978-1-4842-5086-0_2

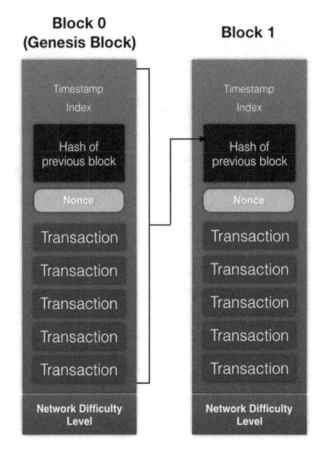

Figure 2-1. *Our conceptual blockchain*

To keep things simple, each block in our blockchain will contain the following components:

- **Timestamp** – the time that the block was added to the blockchain.

- **Index** – a running number starting from 0 indicating the block number.

- **Hash of the previous block** – the hash result of the previous block. As shown in the figure, the hash is the result of hashing the content of the block consisting of the timestamp, index, hash of previous block, nonce, and all the transactions.

- **Nonce** – the *number used once*.

- **Transaction(s)** – each block will hold a variable number of transactions.

Note   For simplicity, we are not going to worry about representing the transactions in a Merkle tree, nor are we going to separate a block into block header and content.

The **network difficulty level** will also be fixed at four zeros – that is, in order to derive the nonce, the result of the hash of the block must start with four zeros.

Tip   Refer to Chapter 1 for the idea behind nonce and how it relates to network difficulty level.

Obtaining the Nonce

For our sample blockchain implementation, the nonce is found by combining it with the index of the block, hash of the previous block, and all the transactions and checking if the resultant hash matches the network difficulty level (see Figure 2-2).

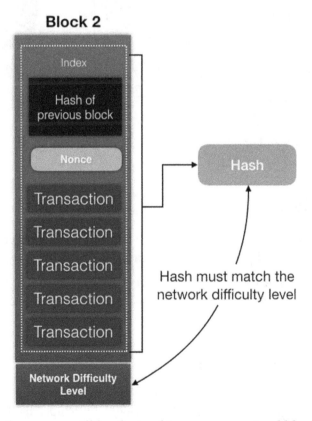

Figure 2-2. *How the nonce will be derived in our conceptual blockchain*

Once the nonce is found, the block will be appended to the last block in the blockchain, with the timestamp added (see Figure 2-3).

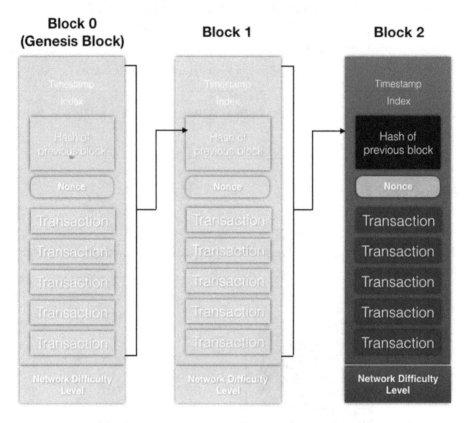

Figure 2-3. *Once a blocked is mined, it will be appended to the blockchain with the timestamp added to the block*

Installing Flask

For our conceptual blockchain, we will run it as a REST API, so that you can interact with it through REST calls. For this, we will use the **Flask** microframework. To install Flask, type the following commands in Terminal:

```
$ pip install flask
$ pip install requests
```

The preceding command installs the Flask microframework.

Tip   Flask is a web framework that makes building web applications easy and rapid.

Importing the Various Modules and Libraries

To get started, let's create a text file named **blockchain.py**. At the top of this file, let's import all the necessary libraries and modules:

```
import sys

import hashlib
import json

from time import time
from uuid import uuid4

from flask import Flask, jsonify, request

import requests
from urllib.parse import urlparse
```

Declaring the Class in Python

To represent the blockchain, let's declare a class named blockchain, with the following two initial methods:

```
class Blockchain(object):

    difficulty_target = "0000"

    def hash_block(self, block):
        block_encoded = json.dumps(block,
            sort_keys=True).encode()
        return hashlib.sha256(block_encoded).hexdigest()

    def __init__(self):
        # stores all the blocks in the entire blockchain
        self.chain = []

        # temporarily stores the transactions for the
        # current block
        self.current_transactions = []
```

```
# create the genesis block with a specific fixed hash
# of previous block genesis block starts with index 0
genesis_hash = self.hash_block("genesis_block")
self.append_block(
    hash_of_previous_block = genesis_hash,
    nonce = self.proof_of_work(0, genesis_hash, [])
)
```

The preceding creates a class named blockchain with two methods:

- The hash_block() method encodes a block into array of bytes and then hashes it; you need to ensure that the dictionary is sorted, or you'll have inconsistent hashes later on

- The __init__() function is the constructor for the class. Here, you store the entire blockchain as a list. Because every blockchain has a genesis block, you need to initialize the genesis block with the hash of the previous block, and in this example, we simply used a fixed string called "genesis_block" to obtain its hash. Once the hash of the previous block is found, we need to find the nonce for the block using the method named proof_of_work() (which we will define in the next section).

The proof_of_work() method (detailed next) will return a nonce that will result in a hash that matches the difficulty target when the content of the current block is hashed.

For simplicity, we are fixing the difficulty_target to a hash result that starts with four zeros ("0000").

Tip   The source code for our blockchain is shown at the end of this chapter. For the impatient, you may wish to look at the code while we go through the various concepts in this chapter.

Finding the Nonce

We now define the proof_of_work() method to find the nonce for the block:

```
# use PoW to find the nonce for the current block
def proof_of_work(self, index, hash_of_previous_block,
transactions):
    # try with nonce = 0
    nonce = 0

    # try hashing the nonce together with the hash of the
    # previous block until it is valid
    while self.valid_proof(index, hash_of_previous_block,
        transactions, nonce) is False:
        nonce += 1

    return nonce
```

The proof_of_work() function first starts with zero for the nonce and check if the nonce together with the content of the block produces a hash that matches the difficulty target. If not, it increments the nonce by one and then try again until it finds the correct nonce.

The next method, valid_proof(), hashes the content of a block and check to see if the block's hash meets the difficulty target:

```
def valid_proof(self, index, hash_of_previous_block,
    transactions, nonce):

    # create a string containing the hash of the previous
    # block and the block content, including the nonce
    content =
f'{index}{hash_of_previous_block}{transactions}{nonce}'.encode()
    # hash using sha256
    content_hash = hashlib.sha256(content).hexdigest()

    # check if the hash meets the difficulty target
    return content_hash[:len(self.difficulty_target)] ==
        self.difficulty_target
```

Appending the Block to the Blockchain

Once the nonce for a block has been found, you can now write the method to append the block to the existing blockchain. This is the function of the append_block() method:

```python
# creates a new block and adds it to the blockchain
def append_block(self, nonce, hash_of_previous_block):
    block = {
        'index': len(self.chain),
        'timestamp': time(),
        'transactions': self.current_transactions,
        'nonce': nonce,
        'hash_of_previous_block': hash_of_previous_block
    }

    # reset the current list of transactions
    self.current_transactions = []

    # add the new block to the blockchain
    self.chain.append(block)
    return block
```

When the block is added to the blockchain, the current timestamp is also added to the block.

Adding Transactions

The next method we will add to the Blockchain class is the add_transaction() method:

```python
def add_transaction(self, sender, recipient, amount):
    self.current_transactions.append({
        'amount': amount,
        'recipient': recipient,
        'sender': sender,
    })
    return self.last_block['index'] + 1
```

This method adds a new transaction to the current list of transactions. It then gets the index of the last block in the blockchain and adds one to it. This new index will be the block that the current transaction will be added to.

To obtain the last block in the blockchain, define a property called last_block in the Blockchain class:

```
@property
def last_block(self):
    # returns the last block in the blockchain
    return self.chain[-1]
```

Exposing the Blockchain Class as a REST API

Our Blockchain class is now complete, and so let's now expose it as a REST API using Flask. Append the following statements to the end of the **blockchain.py** file:

```
app = Flask(__name__)

# generate a globally unique address for this node
node_identifier = str(uuid4()).replace('-', ")

# instantiate the Blockchain
blockchain = Blockchain()
```

Obtaining the Full Blockchain

For the REST API, we want to create a route for users to obtain the current blockchain, so append the following statements to the end of **blockchain.py**:

```
# return the entire blockchain
@app.route('/blockchain', methods=['GET'])
def full_chain():
    response = {
        'chain': blockchain.chain,
        'length': len(blockchain.chain),
    }
    return jsonify(response), 200
```

Performing Mining

We also need to create a route to allow miners to mine a block so that it can be added to the blockchain:

```python
@app.route('/mine', methods=['GET'])
def mine_block():
    blockchain.add_transaction(
        sender="0",
        recipient=node_identifier,
        amount=1,
    )

    # obtain the hash of last block in the blockchain
    last_block_hash = \
        blockchain.hash_block(blockchain.last_block)

    # using PoW, get the nonce for the new block to be added
    # to the blockchain
    index = len(blockchain.chain)
    nonce = blockchain.proof_of_work(index, last_block_hash,
        blockchain.current_transactions)

    # add the new block to the blockchain using the last block
    # hash and the current nonce
    block = blockchain.append_block(nonce, last_block_hash)
    response = {
        'message': "New Block Mined",
        'index': block['index'],
        'hash_of_previous_block':
            block['hash_of_previous_block'],
        'nonce': block['nonce'],
        'transactions': block['transactions'],
    }
    return jsonify(response), 200
```

When a miner managed to mine a block, he must receive a reward for finding the proof. Here, we added a transaction to send one unit of rewards to the miner to signify the rewards for successfully mining the block.

When mining a block, you need to find hash of the previous block and then use it together with the content of the current block to find the nonce for the block. Once the nonce is found, you will append it to the blockchain.

Adding Transactions

Another route that you want to add to the API is the ability to add transactions to the current block:

```
@app.route('/transactions/new', methods=['POST'])
def new_transaction():
    # get the value passed in from the client
    values = request.get_json()

    # check that the required fields are in the POST'ed data
    required_fields = ['sender', 'recipient', 'amount']
    if not all(k in values for k in required_fields):
        return ('Missing fields', 400)

    # create a new transaction
    index = blockchain.add_transaction(
        values['sender'],
        values['recipient'],
        values['amount']
    )

    response = {'message':
        f'Transaction will be added to Block {index}'}
    return (jsonify(response), 201)
```

Examples of transactions are users sending cryptocurrencies from one account to another.

Testing Our Blockchain

We are now ready to test the blockchain. In this final step, add the following statements to the end of **blockchain.py**:

```python
if __name__ == '__main__':
    app.run(host='0.0.0.0', port=int(sys.argv[1]))
```

In this implementation, we allow the user to run the API based on the specified port number.

To start the first node, type the following command in Terminal:

```
$ python blockchain.py 5000
```

You will see the following output:

```
* Serving Flask app "blockchain" (lazy loading)
 * Environment: production
   WARNING: Do not use the development server in a production environment.
   Use a production WSGI server instead.
 * Debug mode: off
 * Running on http://0.0.0.0:5000/ (Press CTRL+C to quit)
```

Our first blockchain running on the first node is now running. It is also listening at port 5000, where you can add transactions to it and mine a block.

In another Terminal window, type the following command to view the content of the blockchain running on the node:

```
$ curl http://localhost:5000/blockchain
```

You will see the following output (formatted for clarity):

```
{
    "chain": [{
        "hash_of_previous_block": "181cfa3e85f3c2a7aa9fb74f992d0d061d3e4a6
        d7461792413aab3f97bd3da95",
        "index": 0,
        "nonce": 61093,
        "timestamp": 1560757569.810427,
        "transactions": []
```

```
    }],
    "length": 1
}
```

Note   The first block (index 0) is the genesis block.

Let's try mining a block to see how it will affect the blockchain. Type the following command in Terminal:

$ **curl http://localhost:5000/mine**

The block that is mined will now be returned:

```
{
    "hash_of_previous_block": "0e8431c4a7fe132503233bc226b1f68c9d2bd4d30af
    24c115bcdad461dda48a0",
    "index": 1,
    "message": "New Block Mined",
    "nonce": 24894,
    "transactions": [{
        "amount": 1,
        "recipient": "084f17b6e5364cde86a231d1cc0c9991",
        "sender": "0"
    }]
}
```

Note   Observe that the block contains a single transaction, which is the reward given to the miner.

You can now issue the command to obtain the blockchain from the node:

$ **curl http://localhost:5000/blockchain**

You will now see that the newly mined block is in the blockchain:

```
{
    "chain": [{
        "hash_of_previous_block": "181cfa3e85f3c2a7aa9fb74f992d0d061d3e4a6d
        7461792413aab3f97bd3da95",
        "index": 0,
        "nonce": 61093,
        "timestamp": 1560757569.810427,
        "transactions": []
    }, {
        "hash_of_previous_block": "0e8431c4a7fe132503233bc226b1f68c9d2bd4d
        30af24c115bcdad461dda48a0",
        "index": 1,
        "nonce": 24894,
        "timestamp": 1560759370.988651,
        "transactions": [{
            "amount": 1,
            "recipient": "084f17b6e5364cde86a231d1cc0c9991",
            "sender": "0"
        }]
    }],
    "length": 2
}
```

Tip   Remember that the default difficulty target is set to four zeros
(difficulty_target = "0000"). You can change it to five zeros and retest the
blockchain. You will realize that it now takes a longer time to mine a block, since it
is more difficult to find a nonce that results in a hash beginning with five zeros.

Let's add a transaction to a block by issuing the following command in Terminal:

```
$    curl -X POST -H "Content-Type: application/json" -d '{
"sender": "04d0988bfa799f7d7ef9ab3de97ef481", "recipient":
"cd0f75d2367ad456607647edde665d6f", "amount": 5}' "http://localhost:5000/
transactions/new"
```

Caution   Note that Windows does not support single quote (') when using curl in the command line. Hence, you need to use double quote and use the slash character (\) to turn off the meaning of double quotes (") in your double-quoted string. The preceding command in Windows would be

```
curl -X POST -H "Content-Type: application/json" -d "{
\"sender\": \"04d0988bfa799f7d7ef9ab3de97ef481\",
\"recipient\": \"cd0f75d2367ad456607647edde665d6f\",
\"amount\": 5}" "http://localhost:5000/transactions/new"
```

You should see the following result:

```
{"message":"Transaction will be added to Block 2"}
```

You can now mine the block:

```
$ curl http://localhost:5000/mine
```

You should see the following result:

```
{
    "hash_of_previous_block": "282991fe48ec07378da72823e6337e13be8524ced51
    00d55c591ae087631146d",
    "index": 2,
    "message": "New Block Mined",
    "nonce": 61520,
    "transactions": [{
        "amount": 5,
        "recipient": "cd0f75d2367ad456607647edde665d6f",
        "sender": "04d0988bfa799f7d7ef9ab3de97ef481"
    }, {
        "amount": 1,
        "recipient": "084f17b6e5364cde86a231d1cc0c9991",
        "sender": "0"
    }]
}
```

The preceding shows that Block 2 has been mined and it contains two transactions – one that you have added manually and another the rewards for the miner.

You can now examine the content of the blockchain by issuing this command:

```
$ curl http://localhost:5000/blockchain
```

You will now see the newly added block containing the two transactions:

```
{
    "chain": [{
        "hash_of_previous_block": "181cfa3e85f3c2a7aa9fb74f992d0d061d3e4a6
        d7461792413aab3f97bd3da95",
        "index": 0,
        "nonce": 61093,
        "timestamp": 1560757569.810427,
        "transactions": []
    }, {
        "hash_of_previous_block": "0e8431c4a7fe132503233bc226b1f68c9d2bd4d3
        0af24c115bcdad461dda48a0",
        "index": 1,
        "nonce": 24894,
        "timestamp": 1560759370.988651,
        "transactions": [{
            "amount": 1,
            "recipient": "084f17b6e5364cde86a231d1cc0c9991",
            "sender": "0"
        }]
    }, {
        "hash_of_previous_block": "282991fe48ec07378da72823e6337e13be8524ce
        d5100d55c591ae087631146d",
        "index": 2,
        "nonce": 61520,
        "timestamp": 1560760629.10675,
        "transactions": [{
            "amount": 5,
            "recipient": "cd0f75d2367ad456607647edde665d6f",
            "sender": "04d0988bfa799f7d7ef9ab3de97ef481"
        }, {
            "amount": 1,
```

```
            "recipient": "084f17b6e5364cde86a231d1cc0c9991",
            "sender": "0"
        }]
    }],
    "length": 3
}
```

Synchronizing Blockchains

In real life, a blockchain network consists of multiple nodes maintaining copies of the same blockchain. So, there must be a way for the nodes to synchronize so that every single node is referring to the same identical blockchain.

When you use Python to run the **blockchain.py** application, only one node is running. The whole idea of blockchain is decentralization – there should be multiple nodes maintaining the blockchain, not just a single one.

For our example, we shall modify it so that each node can be made aware of neighboring nodes on the network (see Figure 2-4).

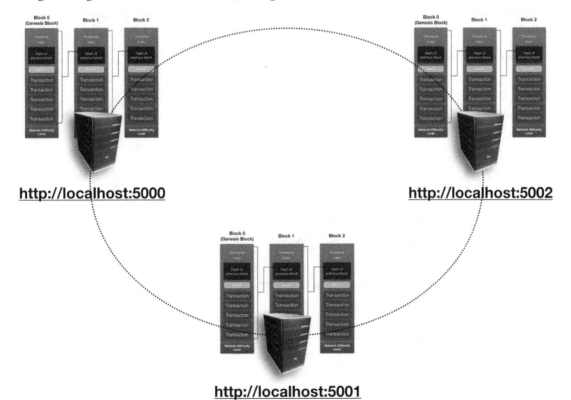

Figure 2-4. *A blockchain network should consist of multiple nodes*

To do that in our example, let's add a number of methods to the Blockchain class. First, add a nodes member to the constructor of the Blockchain class and initialize it to an empty set:

```
def __init__(self):
    self.nodes = set()

    # stores all the blocks in the entire blockchain
    self.chain = []
    ...
```

This nodes member will store the address of other nodes. Next, add a method called add_node() to the Blockchain class:

```
def add_node(self, address):
    parsed_url = urlparse(address)
    self.nodes.add(parsed_url.netloc)
    print(parsed_url.netloc)
```

This method allows a new node to be added to the nodes member, for example, if "http://192.168.0.5:5000" is passed to the method, the IP address and port number "192.168.0.5:5000" will be added to the nodes member.

The next method to add to the Blockchain class is valid_chain():

```
# determine if a given blockchain is valid
def valid_chain(self, chain):

    last_block = chain[0]    # the genesis block
    current_index = 1        # starts with the second block

    while current_index < len(chain):
        block = chain[current_index]
        if block['hash_of_previous_block'] !=
            self.hash_block(last_block):
            return False

        # check for valid nonce
        if not self.valid_proof(
            current_index,
            block['hash_of_previous_block'],
```

```
                 block['transactions'],
                 block['nonce']):
            return False

        # move on to the next block on the chain
        last_block = block
        current_index += 1

    # the chain is valid
    return True
```

The valid_chain() method validates that a given blockchain is valid by performing the following checks:

- It goes through each block in the blockchain and hashes each block and verifies that the hash of each block is correctly recorded in the next block.

- It verifies that the nonce in each block is valid.

Finally, add the update_blockchain() method to the Blockchain class:

```
def update_blockchain(self):
    # get the nodes around us that has been registered
    neighbours = self.nodes
    new_chain = None

    # for simplicity, look for chains longer than ours
    max_length = len(self.chain)

    # grab and verify the chains from all the nodes in our
    # network
    for node in neighbours:
        # get the blockchain from the other nodes
        response =
            requests.get(f'http://{node}/blockchain')

        if response.status_code == 200:
            length = response.json()['length']
            chain = response.json()['chain']
```

```
                    # check if the length is longer and the chain
                    # is valid
                    if length > max_length and
                        self.valid_chain(chain):
                        max_length = length
                        new_chain = chain

            # replace our chain if we discovered a new, valid
            # chain longer than ours
            if new_chain:
                self.chain = new_chain
                return True

        return False
```

The update_blockchain() method works by

- Checking that the blockchain from neighboring nodes is valid and that the node with the longest valid chain is the authoritative one; if another node with a valid blockchain is longer than the current one, it will replace the current blockchain.

With the methods in the Blockchain class defined, you can now define the routes for the REST API:

```
@app.route('/nodes/add_nodes', methods=['POST'])
def add_nodes():
    # get the nodes passed in from the client
    values = request.get_json()
    nodes = values.get('nodes')

    if nodes is None:
        return "Error: Missing node(s) info", 400

    for node in nodes:
        blockchain.add_node(node)

    response = {
        'message': 'New nodes added',
        'nodes': list(blockchain.nodes),
    }
    return jsonify(response), 201
```

The /nodes/add_nodes route allows a node to register one or more neighboring nodes.

The /nodes/sync route allows a node to synchronize its blockchain with its neighboring nodes:

```python
@app.route('/nodes/sync, methods=['GET'])
def sync():
    updated = blockchain.update_blockchain()
    if updated:
        response = {
            'message':
                'The blockchain has been updated to the latest',
            'blockchain': blockchain.chain
        }
    else:
        response = {
            'message': 'Our blockchain is the latest',
            'blockchain': blockchain.chain
        }
    return jsonify(response), 200
```

Testing the Blockchain with Multiple Nodes

In the Terminal that is running the **blockchain.py** application, press Ctrl+C to stop the server. Type the following command to restart it:

```
$ python blockchain.py 5000
```

Open another Terminal window. Type the following command:

```
$ python blockchain.py 5001
```

Tip   You now have two nodes running – one listening at port 5000 and another at 5001.

Let's mine two blocks in the first node (5000) by typing the following commands in *another* Terminal window:

```
$ curl http://localhost:5000/mine
{
    "hash_of_previous_block": "ac46b1f492997e27612a8b5750e0fe340a217aae89e5
    c0efd56959d87127b4d3",
    "index": 1,
    "message": "New Block Mined",
    "nonce": 92305,
    "transactions": [{
        "amount": 1,
        "recipient": "db9ef69db7764331a6f4f23dbb8acd68",
        "sender": "0"
    }]
}
$ curl http://localhost:5000/mine
{
    "hash_of_previous_block": "790ed48f5d52b3eacd2f419e6fdfb2f6b3142bcfc319
    43e4857b7ba4df48bd98",
    "index": 2,
    "message": "New Block Mined",
    "nonce": 224075,
    "transactions": [{
        "amount": 1,
        "recipient": "db9ef69db7764331a6f4f23dbb8acd68",
        "sender": "0"
    }]
}
```

The first node should now have three blocks:

```
$ curl http://localhost:5000/blockchain
{
    "chain": [{
        "hash_of_previous_block": "181cfa3e85f3c2a7aa9fb74f992d0d061d3e4a6d
        7461792413aab3f97bd3da95",
```

```
        "index": 0,
        "nonce": 61093,
        "timestamp": 1560823108.2946198,
        "transactions": []
    }, {
        "hash_of_previous_block": "ac46b1f492997e27612a8b5750e0fe340a217aae
        89e5c0efd56959d87127b4d3",
        "index": 1,
        "nonce": 92305,
        "timestamp": 1560823210.26095,
        "transactions": [{
            "amount": 1,
            "recipient": "db9ef69db7764331a6f4f23dbb8acd68",
            "sender": "0"
        }]
    }, {
        "hash_of_previous_block": "790ed48f5d52b3eacd2f419e6fdfb2f6b3142bcf
        c31943e4857b7ba4df48bd98",
        "index": 2,
        "nonce": 224075,
        "timestamp": 1560823212.887074,
        "transactions": [{
            "amount": 1,
            "recipient": "db9ef69db7764331a6f4f23dbb8acd68",
            "sender": "0"
        }]
    }],
    "length": 3
}
```

As we have not done any mining on the second node (5001), there is only one block in this node:

$ curl http://localhost:5001/blockchain
```
{
    "chain": [{
```

```
        "hash_of_previous_block": "181cfa3e85f3c2a7aa9fb74f992d0d061d3e4a6d
        7461792413aab3f97bd3da95",
        "index": 0,
        "nonce": 61093,
        "timestamp": 1560823126.898498,
        "transactions": []
    }],
    "length": 1
}
```

To tell the second node that there is a neighbor node, use the following command:

```
$ curl -H "Content-type: application/json" -d '{"nodes" :
["http://127.0.0.1:5000"]}' -X POST  http://localhost:5001/nodes/add_nodes
{
    "message": "New nodes added",
    "nodes": ["127.0.0.1:5000"]
}
```

Tip   The preceding command registers a new node with the node at port 5001 that there is a neighboring node listening at port 5000.

To tell the first node that there is a neighbor node, use the following command:

```
$ curl -H "Content-type: application/json" -d '{"nodes" :
["http://127.0.0.1:5001"]}' -X POST  http://localhost:5000/nodes/add_nodes
{
    "message": "New nodes added",
    "nodes": ["127.0.0.1:5001"]
}
```

Tip   The preceding command registers a new node with the node at port 5000 that there is a neighboring node listening at port 5001.

Figure 2-5 shows the two nodes aware of each other's existence.

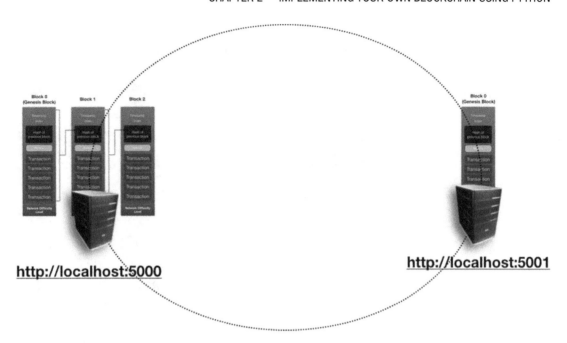

Figure 2-5. *The current states of the two nodes in our blockchain network*

With the first node aware of the existence of the second node (and vice versa), let's try to synchronize the blockchain starting from the first node:

```
$ curl http://localhost:5000/nodes/sync
{
    "blockchain": [{
        "hash_of_previous_block": "181cfa3e85f3c2a7aa9fb74f992d0d061d3e4a6d
        7461792413aab3f97bd3da95",
        "index": 0,
        "nonce": 61093,
        "timestamp": 1560823108.2946198,
        "transactions": []
    }, {
        "hash_of_previous_block": "ac46b1f492997e27612a8b5750e0fe340a217aae
        89e5c0efd56959d87127b4d3",
        "index": 1,
        "nonce": 92305,
        "timestamp": 1560823210.26095,
        "transactions": [{
```

```json
            "amount": 1,
            "recipient": "db9ef69db7764331a6f4f23dbb8acd68",
            "sender": "0"
        }]
    }, {
        "hash_of_previous_block": "790ed48f5d52b3eacd2f419e6fdfb2f6b3142bcf
        c31943e4857b7ba4df48bd98",
        "index": 2,
        "nonce": 224075,
        "timestamp": 1560823212.887074,
        "transactions": [{
            "amount": 1,
            "recipient": "db9ef69db7764331a6f4f23dbb8acd68",
            "sender": "0"
        }]
    }],
    "message": "Our blockchain is the latest"
}
```

As the result shows, the first node has the longest chain (three blocks), and hence the blockchain is the latest, and it remains intact. We now synchronize from the second node:

```
$ curl http://localhost:5001/nodes/sync
{
    "blockchain": [{
        "hash_of_previous_block": "181cfa3e85f3c2a7aa9fb74f992d0d061d3e4a6d
        7461792413aab3f97bd3da95",
        "index": 0,
        "nonce": 61093,
        "timestamp": 1560823108.2946198,
        "transactions": []
    }, {
        "hash_of_previous_block": "ac46b1f492997e27612a8b5750e0fe340a217aae
        89e5c0efd56959d87127b4d3",
        "index": 1,
```

```
        "nonce": 92305,
        "timestamp": 1560823210.26095,
        "transactions": [{
            "amount": 1,
            "recipient": "db9ef69db7764331a6f4f23dbb8acd68",
            "sender": "0"
        }]
    }, {
        "hash_of_previous_block": "790ed48f5d52b3eacd2f419e6fdfb2f6b3142bcf
        c31943e4857b7ba4df48bd98",
        "index": 2,
        "nonce": 224075,
        "timestamp": 1560823212.887074,
        "transactions": [{
            "amount": 1,
            "recipient": "db9ef69db7764331a6f4f23dbb8acd68",
            "sender": "0"
        }]
    }],
    "message": "The blockchain has been updated to the latest"
}
```

As the second node's blockchain only has one block, it is therefore deemed outdated. It now replaces its blockchain from that of the first node.

Full Listing for the Python Blockchain Implementation

```python
import sys

import hashlib
import json

from time import time
from uuid import uuid4

from flask import Flask, jsonify, request
```

```python
import requests
from urllib.parse import urlparse

class Blockchain(object):

    difficulty_target = "0000"

    def hash_block(self, block):
        # encode the block into bytes and then hashes it;
        # ensure that the dictionary is sorted, or you'll
        # have inconsistent hashes
        block_encoded = json.dumps(block,
            sort_keys=True).encode()
        return hashlib.sha256(block_encoded).hexdigest()

    def __init__(self):
        self.nodes = set()

        # stores all the blocks in the entire blockchain
        self.chain = []

        # temporarily stores the transactions for the current
        # block
        self.current_transactions = []

        # create the genesis block with a specific fixed hash
        # of previous block genesis block starts with index 0
        genesis_hash = self.hash_block("genesis_block")
        self.append_block(
            hash_of_previous_block = genesis_hash,
            nonce = self.proof_of_work(0, genesis_hash, [])
        )

    # use PoW to find the nonce for the current block
    def proof_of_work(self, index, hash_of_previous_block,
        transactions):
        # try with nonce = 0
        nonce = 0

        # try hashing the nonce together with the hash of the
```

```python
        # previous block until it is valid
        while self.valid_proof(index, hash_of_previous_block,
            transactions, nonce) is False:
            nonce += 1

        return nonce

    # check if the block's hash meets the difficulty target
    def valid_proof(self, index, hash_of_previous_block,
        transactions, nonce):

        # create a string containing the hash of the previous
        # block and the block content, including the nonce
        content =
f'{index}{hash_of_previous_block}{transactions}{nonce}'.encode()

        # hash using sha256
        content_hash = hashlib.sha256(content).hexdigest()

        # check if the hash meets the difficulty target
        return content_hash[:len(self.difficulty_target)] ==
            self.difficulty_target

    # creates a new block and adds it to the blockchain
    def append_block(self, nonce, hash_of_previous_block):
        block = {
            'index': len(self.chain),
            'timestamp': time(),
            'transactions': self.current_transactions,
            'nonce': nonce,
            'hash_of_previous_block': hash_of_previous_block
        }

        # reset the current list of transactions
        self.current_transactions = []

        # add the new block to the blockchain
        self.chain.append(block)
        return block
```

```python
    def add_transaction(self, sender, recipient, amount):
        # adds a new transaction to the current list of
        # transactions
        self.current_transactions.append({
            'amount': amount,
            'recipient': recipient,
            'sender': sender,
        })
        # get the index of the last block in the blockchain
        # and add one to it this will be the block that the
        # current transaction will be added to
        return self.last_block['index'] + 1

    @property
    def last_block(self):
        # returns the last block in the blockchain
        return self.chain[-1]

    # --------------------
    # add a new node to the list of nodes e.g.
    # 'http://192.168.0.5:5000'
    def add_node(self, address):
        parsed_url = urlparse(address)
        self.nodes.add(parsed_url.netloc)
        print(parsed_url.netloc)

    # determine if a given blockchain is valid
    def valid_chain(self, chain):

        last_block = chain[0]    # the genesis block
        current_index = 1        # starts with the second block

        while current_index < len(chain):
            # get the current block
            block = chain[current_index]

            # check that the hash of the previous block is
            # correct by hashing the previous block and then
```

```
        # comparing it with the one recorded in the
        # current block
        if block['hash_of_previous_block'] !=
            self.hash_block(last_block):
            return False

        # check that the nonce is correct by hashing the
        # hash of the previous block together with the
        # nonce and see if it matches the target
        if not self.valid_proof(
            current_index,
            block['hash_of_previous_block'],
            block['transactions'],
            block['nonce']):
            return False

        # move on to the next block on the chain
        last_block = block
        current_index += 1

    # the chain is valid
    return True

def update_blockchain(self):
    # get the nodes around us that has been registered
    neighbours = self.nodes
    new_chain = None

    # for simplicity, look for chains longer than ours
    max_length = len(self.chain)

    # grab and verify the chains from all the nodes in
    # our network
    for node in neighbours:
        # get the blockchain from the other nodes
        response =
            requests.get(f'http://{node}/blockchain')

        if response.status_code == 200:
```

```python
                length = response.json()['length']
                chain = response.json()['chain']

                # check if the length is longer and the chain
                # is valid
                if length > max_length and
                    self.valid_chain(chain):
                    max_length = length
                    new_chain = chain

        # replace our chain if we discovered a new, valid
        # chain longer than ours
        if new_chain:
            self.chain = new_chain
            return True

        return False

app = Flask(__name__)

# generate a globally unique address for this node
node_identifier = str(uuid4()).replace('-', ")

# instantiate the Blockchain
blockchain = Blockchain()

# return the entire blockchain
@app.route('/blockchain', methods=['GET'])
def full_chain():
    response = {
        'chain': blockchain.chain,
        'length': len(blockchain.chain),
    }
    return jsonify(response), 200

@app.route('/mine', methods=['GET'])
def mine_block():
    # the miner must receive a reward for finding the proof
```

```python
    # the sender is "0" to signify that this node has mined a
    # new coin.
    blockchain.add_transaction(
        sender="0",
        recipient=node_identifier,
        amount=1,
    )

    # obtain the hash of last block in the blockchain
    last_block_hash =
        blockchain.hash_block(blockchain.last_block)

    # using PoW, get the nonce for the new block to be added
    # to the blockchain
    index = len(blockchain.chain)
    nonce = blockchain.proof_of_work(index, last_block_hash,
        blockchain.current_transactions)

    # add the new block to the blockchain using the last block
    # hash and the current nonce
    block = blockchain.append_block(nonce, last_block_hash)
    response = {
        'message': "New Block Mined",
        'index': block['index'],
        'hash_of_previous_block':
            block['hash_of_previous_block'],
        'nonce': block['nonce'],
        'transactions': block['transactions'],
    }
    return jsonify(response), 200

@app.route('/transactions/new', methods=['POST'])
def new_transaction():
    # get the value passed in from the client
    values = request.get_json()

    # check that the required fields are in the POST'ed data
    required_fields = ['sender', 'recipient', 'amount']
```

```python
    if not all(k in values for k in required_fields):
        return ('Missing fields', 400)

    # create a new transaction
    index = blockchain.add_transaction(
        values['sender'],
        values['recipient'],
        values['amount']
    )

    response = {'message':
        f'Transaction will be added to Block {index}'}
    return (jsonify(response), 201)

@app.route('/nodes/add_nodes', methods=['POST'])
def add_nodes():
    # get the nodes passed in from the client
    values = request.get_json()
    nodes = values.get('nodes')

    if nodes is None:
        return "Error: Missing node(s) info", 400

    for node in nodes:
        blockchain.add_node(node)

    response = {
        'message': 'New nodes added',
        'nodes': list(blockchain.nodes),
    }
    return jsonify(response), 201

@app.route('/nodes/sync', methods=['GET'])
def sync():
    updated = blockchain.update_blockchain()
    if updated:
        response = {
            'message':
                'The blockchain has been updated to the latest',
```

```
            'blockchain': blockchain.chain
        }
    else:
        response = {
            'message': 'Our blockchain is the latest',
            'blockchain': blockchain.chain
        }
    return jsonify(response), 200

if __name__ == '__main__':
    app.run(host='0.0.0.0', port=int(sys.argv[1]))
```

Summary

In this chapter, you learned how to build your own blockchain using Python. Through this exercise, you learned how

- Blocks are added to the blockchain

- The nonce in a block is found

- To synchronize blockchains between nodes

In the next chapter, you will learn how to connect to the real blockchain – the Ethereum blockchain.

## CHAPTER 3

Connecting to the Ethereum Blockchain

Now that you have a solid understanding of how a blockchain works, you are ready to connect to the real Ethereum blockchain. To get connected to the Ethereum blockchain, you need an Ethereum client – an application that runs as an Ethereum node on the blockchain. Using an Ethereum client, you can perform tasks such as the following:

- Mine Ethers.

- Transfer Ethers from one account to another.

- View block information.

- Create and deploy Smart Contracts.

- Use and interact with Smart Contracts.

At the time of writing, there are a number of Ethereum clients that you can use to interact with the Ethereum blockchain. They are

- **Eth** – A C++ Ethereum client

- **Geth** – The official Ethereum client implemented using the Go programming language

- **Pyethapp** – A Python Ethereum client

- **Parity** – An Ethereum client written using the Rust programming language

The preceding list are all CLI (command line interface) clients. If you want to use a GUI client, you can use **Mist**, which is built on top of **Geth**. For this book, we shall focus on the use of Geth.

© Wei-Meng Lee 2019
W.-M. Lee, *Beginning Ethereum Smart Contracts Programming,*
https://doi.org/10.1007/978-1-4842-5086-0_3

Downloading and Installing Geth

Geth is available for three main paltforms:

- Linux

- macOS

- Windows

Also, the sources of Geth is also available for download at https://geth.ethereum. org/downloads/ if you want to learn how Geth is implemented. In the following sections, I will show you how to download and install Geth for the three main platforms.

Installing Geth for macOS

There are two ways to install Geth for macOS. The first is through the command line. To do that, you need to use **Brew**.

Tip Homebrew (commonly known as Brew) is a free and open-source software package management system that simplifies the installation of software on Apple's macOS operating system and Linux.

If you do not have Brew, you need to install it first. To do so, in Terminal, type the following command to install Brew:

```
$ /usr/bin/ruby -e "$(curl -fsSL https://raw.githubusercontent.com/
Homebrew/install/master/install)"
```

Then type the following commands to update and upgrade Brew:

```
$ brew update
$ brew upgrade
```

To install Geth in Terminal, type the following commands in Terminal:

```
$ brew tap ethereum/Ethereum
$ brew install ethereum
```

Tip   To upgrade Geth to the latest version, use the following command: `brew upgrade Ethereum`. To find out the current version of Geth you have installed on your computer, use the command: `geth help`.

If you do not want to install Geth from Terminal, the second way to install Geth is to go to `https://geth.ethereum.org/downloads/` and download Geth for macOS (see Figure 3-1).

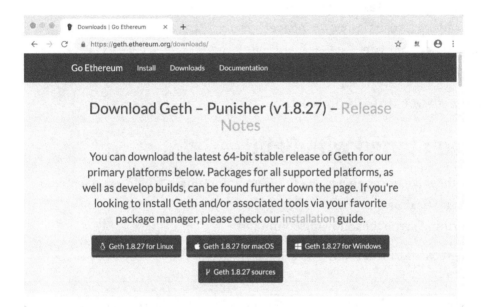

Figure 3-1. *Downloading Geth from its web site*

Once downloaded, unzip the file and move the `Geth` file onto your home directory.

Installing Geth for Windows

For Windows user, the easiest way to install Geth is to go to `https://geth.ethereum.org/downloads/` and click the button for the Windows version of Geth.

Once downloaded, double-click the .exe to install Geth on your Windows machine.

Tip   For Windows users, if you encounter problems in running any of the commands in this book, you should use the PowerShell instead of the Command Prompt.

Installing Geth for Linux

For Linux user, you can install Geth by downloading the version of Geth for Linux from https://geth.ethereum.org/downloads/, and unzip the file and move the geth file onto your home directory.

Alternatively, you can also install Geth through Terminal. In Terminal, type the following commands:

```
$ sudo apt-get install software-properties-common
$ sudo add-apt-repository -y ppa:ethereum/ethereum
$ sudo apt-get update
$ sudo apt-get install ethereum
```

And Geth would now be installed.

Getting Started with Geth

Using Geth, you can connect to the Ethereum blockchain and interact with it. Let's see how this can be done.

In Terminal, type the following command:

```
$ geth --testnet --datadir ~/.ethereum-testnet
```

Note   All the commands and examples in this book will be based on macOS.

Here is what the preceding command means:

- The geth client will attempt to connect to the **Ropsten** test network (--testnet) and download the entire blockchain from the network.

    - If you want to connect to another test network called **Rinkeby**, use the --rinkeby option.

- The --datadir option specifies the local storage to use to store the blockchain, keystore, and other local client data (in this example, it is stored in a hidden folder named .ethereum-testnet in your home directory).

The entire blockchain for the network will now be downloaded onto your computer; in this case it will be saved in the ~/.ethereum-testnet directory.

ETHEREUM NETWORKS

Apart from the Main Ethereum Network (known as *mainnet*), Ethereum has a number of test networks (known as *testnets*) that you can use for development purposes. The beauty of the testnets is that the Ether on these networks has no real monetary value, and hence you can test and explore the Ethereum blockchain to your hearts content. Only when you are finally done with your testing (and learning) do you need to connect to the mainnet for real-life deployment. At the time of writing, there are four testnets:

- Ropsten

- Kovan

- Rinkeby

- Goerli

Examining the Data Downloaded

The Geth is going to take some time to download the entire blockchain onto your computer (up to a few days depending on your connection speed). In the meantime, you can take a look at the folders created by Geth in the ~/.ethereum-testnet directory. You should see two folders as shown in Figure 3-2.

Figure 3-2. Examining the folders created by Geth

The **geth** folder contains the blockchain that you are downloading, while the **keystore** folder contains the account details of your local Ethereum node. We will discuss these in more details in the next chapter.

Tip   It will take Geth quite a bit of time to synchronize all the data to the computer. At the time of writing (June 2019), the size of the Ethereum mainnet is about 250GB. So, if you are synchronizing with the mainnet, make sure you have enough disk space. You can check for the size of the various cryptocurrencies blockchain size at `https://bitinfocharts.com`.

Geth JavaScript Console

Observe that when Geth is running, all you see is text after text scrolling (these are the statuses of the synchronization). It would be more useful if you are able to interact with Geth directly. And this is possible through the **Geth JavaScript Console**.

To use the Geth JavaScript Console, add the following option in bold to the Geth command in the Terminal:

```
$ geth --testnet --datadir ~/.ethereum-testnet console 2>console.log
```

You should now see a prompt (>) after issuing this command:

```
$ geth --testnet --datadir ~/.ethereum-testnet console 2>console.log
Welcome to the Geth JavaScript console!

instance: Geth/v1.8.27-stable/darwin-amd64/go1.12.4
 modules: admin:1.0 debug:1.0 eth:1.0 ethash:1.0 miner:1.0 net:1.0
 personal:1.0 rpc:1.0 txpool:1.0 web3:1.0

>
```

The Command Prompt allows you to issue JavaScript commands (hence its name), such as `personal.newAccount()`, which allows you to create a new account in the current node:

```
> personal.newAccount()
Passphrase: <password>
Repeat passphrase: <password>
"0x9ba59863c7d2e62c6f63baefb45a96b61bcb03ee"
```

Note   We will discuss more Geth commands in the next chapter.

If you want to run Geth in a separate window without the Geth JavaScript Console but at the same time want to interact with Geth, you can run Geth with the following options:

```
$ geth --testnet --datadir ~/.ethereum-testnet --rpc --rpcport 8545
```

The `--rpc` option enables the HTTP_RPC server, and the `--rpcport 8545` option means that the HTTP_RPC server is listening at port 8545 to allow other clients to connect to it.

In another Terminal window, you can connect to the Geth node using the `attach` option:

```
$ geth attach http://127.0.0.1:8545
```

Once connected, you will see the following:

```
Welcome to the Geth JavaScript console!

instance: Geth/v1.8.22-stable/darwin-amd64/go1.11.5
 modules: eth:1.0 net:1.0 rpc:1.0 web3:1.0

>
```

To exit the Geth JavaScript Console, use the `exit` command:

```
> exit
```

Sync Modes

Geth supports three sync modes:

- Full node mode (with fast synchronization) – When you launch the Geth client without specifying the --syncmode option, the default mode used by Geth is **Full Nodes with Fast Synchronization** (--syncmode fast). In Full node mode, Geth will download the full blockchain onto your computer by first downloading the block headers first and filling in block bodies and receipts afterward. Once the fast sync reached the last block of the Ethereum network, it switches to a full sync mode (see next point). It also validates the latest.

- Full node mode – Synchronizes a full node starting at the genesis block and verifying all blocks and executing all transactions. This mode is slower than the fast sync mode but comes with increased security.

- Light node mode – A light node only downloads the header chain and requests everything else on-demand from the network. They can verify the validity of the data against the state roots in the block headers. To use the light node mode, use the --syncmode light option.

When performing a sync using Geth, you can know the state of the synchronization using the eth.syncing property:

```
> web3.eth.syncing
{
  currentBlock: 5529791,
  highestBlock: 5653493,
  knownStates: 0,
  pulledStates: 0,
  startingBlock: 5308415
}
```

The preceding output indicates that the syncing starts from block number 5308415 and the current block number is 5529791. The highest block number is 5653493. If you get a `false` from the `eth.syncing` property, this means that syncing is not performed at the moment.

At any point in time, you can always check the latest block number that has been synchronized on your local node using the `eth.blockNumber` property, like this:

```
> eth.blockNumber
5653597
```

Summary

In this chapter, you learned how to download and install Geth, an Ethereum client, on the various platforms. In the next chapter, you will learn how to use Geth to set up a private test network so that you can use it to build your own blockchain network.

CHAPTER 4

Creating Your Own Private Ethereum Test Network

In the previous chapter, you saw how to download and install the *Geth* client. You also saw how to connect to the various Ethereum networks and how to examine the blockchain using the blockchain explorer – EtherScan.

One useful feature of *Geth* is that you can use it to create your own private test network in your local setup, without connecting to the real blockchain. This makes the development work much easier and allow you to explore the Ethereum blockchain without needing to pay for real Ether. Hence, in this chapter you will see how you can create your own private Ethereum test network, as well as how to connect to peers and perform transactions such as sending Ethers between accounts.

Creating the Private Ethereum Test Network

For this example, we are going to create a private test network comprising of two nodes in a single computer – **node1** and **node2**, and a third node – **node3**, on another computer (see Figure 4-1).

© Wei-Meng Lee 2019
W.-M. Lee, *Beginning Ethereum Smart Contracts Programming*,
https://doi.org/10.1007/978-1-4842-5086-0_4

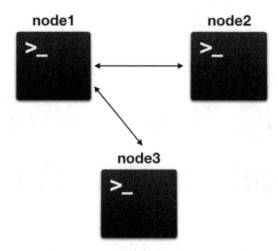

Figure 4-1. *Our private Ethereum test network*

These three nodes will form your own test network where you can do things like mining, transferring Ethers to another account, and in the next chapter, deploy your Smart Contracts.

Creating the Genesis Block

Before you proceed to create your own private Ethereum test network, you need to create the *genesis block*. The genesis block is the start of the blockchain – the first block (block 0), and the only block that does not point to a predecessor block. The Ethereum protocol ensures that no other node will agree with your version of the blockchain unless they have the same genesis block, so you can make as many private testnet blockchains as you'd like.

For this chapter, you will create a folder named **MyTestNet** on your computer. For simplicity, I will create this folder in my home directory:

```
$ cd ~
$ mkdir MyTestNet
$ cd MyTestNet
```

For Windows users, the home directory is typically C:\users*<user_name>*\.

To create the genesis block, create a file named **genesisblock.json** and populate it as follows:

```
{
  "config": {
        "chainId": 10,
        "homesteadBlock": 0,
        "eip155Block": 0,
        "eip158Block": 0
    },
  "alloc"      : {},
  "coinbase"   : "0x0000000000000000000000000000000000000000",
  "difficulty" : "0x20000",
  "extraData"  : "",
  "gasLimit"   : "0x2fefd8",
  "nonce"      : "0x0000000000000042",
  "mixhash"    : "0x0000000000000000000000000000000000000000000000000000000000
                  000000000",
  "parentHash" : "0x0000000000000000000000000000000000000000000000000000000000
                  000000000",
  "timestamp"  : "0x00"
}
```

Creating a Folder for Storing Node Data

Next, you need to create a directory to store the data for all the nodes in your private test network. For this, we shall create a directory named **data** in the **MyTestNet** folder:

```
$ cd ~/MyTestNet
$ mkdir data
```

Figure 4-2 shows the directory structure at this point.

Figure 4-2. *The content of the MyTestNet directory*

Initiating a Blockchain Node

To create a node on the test network, you need to initialize it using the genesis block you have created earlier. You can do it using the following command:

```
$ geth --datadir ~/MyTestNet/data/node1 init
~/MyTestNet/genesisblock.json
```

The preceding creates a node named **node1** and saves all its data in the **node1** directory. You should see the following response:

```
INFO [01-08|13:11:00.937] Maximum peer count
ETH=25 LES=0 total=25
INFO [01-08|13:11:00.947] Allocated cache and file handles
database=/Users/weimenglee/MyTestNet/data/node1/geth/chaindata cache=16
handles=16
INFO [01-08|13:11:00.950] Writing custom genesis block
INFO [01-08|13:11:00.950] Persisted trie from memory database
nodes=0 size=0.00B time=11.47µs gcnodes=0 gcsize=0.00B gctime=0s
livenodes=1 livesize=0.00B
INFO [01-08|13:11:00.950] Successfully wrote genesis state
database=chaindata
hash=5e1fc7...d790e0
INFO [01-08|13:11:00.950] Allocated cache and file handles
database=/Users/weimenglee/MyTestNet/data/node1/geth/lightchaindata
cache=16 handles=16
INFO [01-08|13:11:00.952] Writing custom genesis block
INFO [01-08|13:11:00.952] Persisted trie from memory database
nodes=0 size=0.00B time=1.856µs gcnodes=0 gcsize=0.00B gctime=0s
livenodes=1 livesize=0.00B
INFO [01-08|13:11:00.952] Successfully wrote genesis state
database=lightchaindata
hash=5e1fc7...d790e0
```

Figure 4-3 shows the content of **node1** after this command is run.

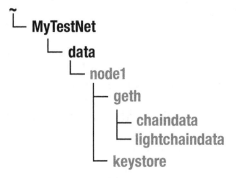

Figure 4-3. *The content of the node1 directory*

The **Geth** directory contains two folders for storing the blockchains – **chaindata** and **lightchaindata**, while the **keystore** directory contains accounts information (more on this later).

Let's create another node, this time let's call it **node2**:

```
$ geth --datadir ~/MyTestNet/data/node2 init
~/MyTestNet/genesisblock.json
```

Figure 4-4 shows the current state of the **MyTestNet** directory.

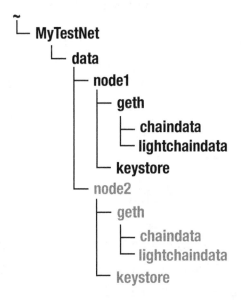

Figure 4-4. *The node2 directory is now added to the data directory*

Starting Up the Nodes

Now that the nodes have been initialized, let's start them up. Let's start up **node1**:

```
$ geth --datadir ~/MyTestNet/data/node1 console 2>console1.log
```

Once **node1** is started up, you will see the *Geth JavaScript Console*:

```
Welcome to the Geth JavaScript console!

instance: Geth/v1.8.20-stable/darwin-amd64/go1.11.4
 modules: admin:1.0 debug:1.0 eth:1.0 ethash:1.0 miner:1.0 net:1.0
personal:1.0 rpc:1.0 txpool:1.0 web3:1.0

>
```

Tip   The *Geth JavaScript Console* provides an interactive console for you to interact with the Ethereum blockchain using the JavaScript language.

The console 2 option basically redirects the output to a file (named console1.log in this example). Without this redirection, *Geth* would continually generate a lot of output and the Geth JavaScript Console would not be usable.

Creating Accounts

Now that **node1** is started up, you can create a new account in your node using the personal.newAccount() function:

```
> personal.newAccount()
Passphrase: <password>
Repeat passphrase: <password>
"0xe225dc6b5e85b6f2659ca310b2a17247291e6b6b"
```

The web3 object (from the web3.js library) allows you to programmatically interact with the Ethereum blockchain. It also exposes the eth object, which itself also exposes the personal object. Hence the full name for the personal.newAccount() function is actually web3.eth.personal.newAccount(). The personal object allows you to interact with the Ethereum node's accounts.

You can be asked to enter a password for the new account. Once that is done, the public address of the account is displayed.

To show the list of accounts in your node, use the `eth.accounts` property:

```
> eth.accounts
["0xe225dc6b5e85b6f2659ca310b2a17247291e6b6b"]
```

The list of accounts will be shown as an array. In the example here, there is only one account.

Once the account is created, you will be able to find the account details stored in a file (named beginning with the UTC word) in the ~/**MyTestNet/data/node1/keystore** directory. We will talk more about this later in this chapter.

Checking the Balance of an Account

To check the balance of an account, use the `eth.getBalance()` function:

```
> eth.getBalance(eth.accounts[0])
0
```

As mentioned earlier, the `eth` object is derived from the `web3` object, so the preceding function is equivalent to `web3.eth.getBalance(web3.eth.accounts[0])`.

Apparently, at this moment has no ethers, so you will see a 0. However, do note that the unit displayed for the balance is *Wei*, where 1 Ether is 1000000000000000000 Wei (1 followed by 18 zeros). Very often, you do not want to see the units displayed in *Wei* but rather in *Ether*. To make your life easier, you can use the `web3.fromWei()` function, like the following command, to convert the balance in Wei to Ether:

```
> web3.fromWei(eth.getBalance(eth.accounts[0]), "ether")
0
```

Table 4-1 shows the different units in Ethereum.

Table 4-1. *Units in Ethereum*

Unit	Wei Value	Wei
wei	1 wei	1
Kwei (babbage)	10^3 wei	1,000
Mwei (lovelace)	10^6 wei	1,000,000
Gwei (shannon)	10^9 wei	1,000,000,000
microether (szabo)	10^{12} wei	1,000,000,000,000
milliether (finney)	10^{15} wei	1,000,000,000,000,000
ether	10^{18} wei	1,000,000,000,000,000,000

Stopping the Node

To stop the node, simply use the exit command:

```
> exit
```

For now, let's stop **node1**.

Starting Another Node

Now that we have started **node1** and then stopped it, let's now start **node2**. In a new Terminal window, type the following command:

```
$ geth --datadir ~/MyTestNet/data/node2 --port 30304
--nodiscover --networkid 2345 console 2>console2.log
```

Observe that in the preceding command, I have specified the --port option and set the port to 30304. This is because *Geth* by default uses port 30303, and if you have multiple nodes running on the same computer, each node must use a unique port number. By setting this to port 30304, it will prevent conflicting with another node using the default port. The --nodiscover option means that peers will not automatically discover each other and that they need to be added manually. The --networkid option specifies the network id so that other nodes can attach to the network with the same network id.

Once **node2** is started, restart **node1** with the following command:

```
$ geth --datadir ~/MyTestNet/data/node1 --networkid 2345
console 2>console1.log
```

Notice that **node1** is started with the --networkid option with the value of 2345. This is required so that it can be added as a peer to **node2** later on. Figure 4-5 shows the state of the two nodes at this moment.

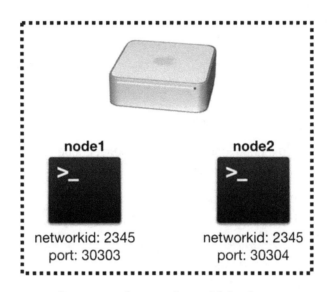

Figure 4-5. *The two nodes currently running within the same computer*

Getting Information About the Node

Now that the two nodes are up and running, let's get some detailed information about each of them. Type the following command in **node1**:

```
> admin.nodeInfo
{
  enode:  "enode://177be9b5b6beb0fb045bb35e5dea443016187fb0d7fdddbcce4b520d5
          54ec4345a4f07702bca8ca0204107612ba39ae5115257350b5b31174239ad5916
          8312aa@138.75.206.153:30303",
  enr:  "0xf896b84076d1c710e54b570ae6f96ed94cadce07025e89d0b178ef82d97f78ed0
          0cab1bf0e0c752c86eb7cafce38cc538114eb3284a37e7b1267283c4d9bd292b49e
          289f0383636170c6c5836574683f826964827634826970848a4bce9989736563703
```

```
        235366b31a102177be9b5b6beb0fb045bb35e5dea443016187fb0d7fdddbcce4b52
        0d554ec4348374637082765f8375647082765f",
  id: "142e0fc58a6598b51d9f5ecdee56e60836a9cd58e7717234df3e6514f84ffc03",
  ip: "138.75.206.153",
  listenAddr: "[::]:30303",
  name: "Geth/v1.8.20-stable/darwin-amd64/go1.11.4",
  ports: {
    discovery: 30303,
    listener: 30303
  },
  protocols: {
    eth: {
      config: {
        chainId: 10,
        eip150Hash: "0x0000000000000000000000000000000000000000000000000000
                    000000000000",
        eip155Block: 0,
        eip158Block: 0,
        homesteadBlock: 0
      },
      difficulty: 131072,
      genesis: "0x5e1fc79cb4ffa4739177b5408045cd5d51c6cf766133f23f7cd72ee1f
      8d790e0",
      head: "0x5e1fc79cb4ffa4739177b5408045cd5d51c6cf766133f23f7cd72ee1f8d7
      90e0",
      network: 2345
    }
  }
}
```

The `admin` object is derived from the `web3` object. Hence the full name of `admin.addPeer()` is `web3.admin.addPeer()`. The `admin` object allows you to interact with the underlying blockchain.

You will a whole bunch of information. In particular, take note of the preceding enode key (bolded for emphasis). At the end of the enode value, observe the port number 30303 (which is the port node 1 is using).

Tip   An enode describes a node in the Ethereum network in the form of an URI.

Pairing the Nodes

Copy the value of the enode key in **node1**, and in **node2**, type the following command:

> **admin.addPeer("*enode://177be9b5b6beb0fb045bb35e5dea443016187fb0d7*
fdddbcce4b520d554ec4345a4f07702bca8ca0204107612ba39ae51152
57350b5b31174239ad59168312aa@138.75.206.153:30303")**

Caution   In the preceding example, the **138.75.206.153** refers to my computer's public IP address. When pairing with another node on the same computer/network, it is important to replace this IP address with that of the local IP address of the computer. If you don't do this, the two nodes will not be paired correctly.

In the preceding command, the bolded portion is the value of the enode key of **node1**. The admin.addPeer() function adds a peer to the current node using the peer's enode value.

To verify that the peer is added successfully, use the admin.peers property:

```
> admin.peers
[{
    caps: ["eth/63"],
    enode: "enode://177be9b5b6beb0fb045bb35e5dea443016187fb0d7fdddbcce4b520
            d554ec4345a4f07702bca8ca0204107612ba39ae5115257350b5b31174239ad
            59168312aa@138.75.206.153:30303",
    id: "142e0fc58a6598b51d9f5ecdee56e60836a9cd58e7717234df3e6514f84ffc03",
    name: "Geth/v1.8.20-stable/darwin-amd64/go1.11.4",
    network: {
      inbound: false,
      localAddress: "192.168.1.116:63908",
```

```
    remoteAddress: "138.75.206.153:30303",
    static: true,
    trusted: false
  },
  protocols: {
    eth: {
      difficulty: 131072,
      head: "0x5e1fc79cb4ffa4739177b5408045cd5d51c6cf766133f23f7cd72ee1f8
      d790e0",
      version: 63
    }
  }
}]
```

If the peer is added successfully, you should see the preceding output. From the output, you can see that the **node1**'s IP address is 192.168.1.116, which is the IP address of my computer. Figure 4-6 shows the current state of our private test network.

The admin.peers property returns a [ ] if there is currently no peer attached to the node.

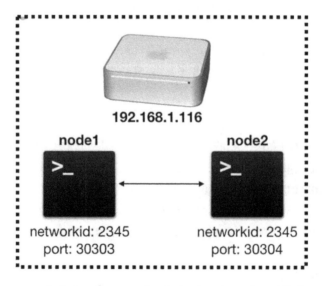

Figure 4-6. *The current state of our private test network, with two peered nodes*

So far, we have been pairing the nodes within the same computer. How do you pair nodes from another computer?

Note   I will leave the creation of the third node as an exercise for the reader.

Suppose you have another node – **node3**, running on another computer. On the Geth JavaScript Console on that node, you can add **node1** as a peer by using the following command:

```
> admin.addPeer("enode://177be9b5b6beb0fb045bb35e5dea443016
187fb0d7fdddbcce4b520d554ec4345a4f07702bca8ca0204107612ba39
ae5115257350b5b31174239ad59168312aa@192.168.1.116:30303")
```

You just need to replace the IP address and port number of the node with that of the node you are trying to add to. In this example, **node1** is running on port 30303, and its IP address is 192.168.1.116. Figure 4-7 summarizes the state of the nodes at this moment.

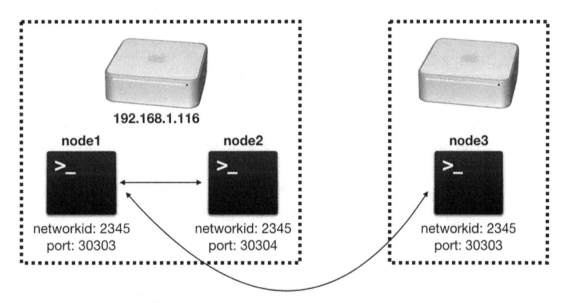

Figure 4-7. *Our private test network with three connected nodes*

Performing Mining

With all the nodes connected, we can start to perform some mining operations! Before we do that, let's verify the block numbers for the current blockchain. In any of the nodes, you can use the `eth.blockNumber` property to display the latest block number in the blockchain:

```
> eth.blockNumber
0
```

As expected, we should see 0. This is because at this moment the blockchain has only one block – the genesis block. To start the mining on **node1**, use the `miner.start()` function:

```
> miner.start(1)
null
```

The number you passed into the start() function is the number of threads you want to use for the mining operation. Don't be alarmed with the null result. The null simply means that the function has nothing to return to you; it does not indicate the failure of the mining operation.

Note   The `miner` object is derived from the `web3` object.

The **node1** will now start the mining operation. On some computers, it will take a few minutes to mine the first block, while on some slower machines, it will take a much longer time. So be patient.

You can verify that a block has been mined by checking the result of the `eth.blockNumber` property. If the block number is more than 0, then you have mined your first block! Congratulations!

And since **node2** is connected to **node1**, you can also verify the block number in **node2**. You should see the same block number.

Caution   If **node2** is not seeing the same block number as **node1**, it means that the two are not paired up correctly.

If you need to stop the mining, you can use the `miner.stop()` function. For now, leave the mining on.

Tip   This is a good time to check the balance of your account. If you have managed to mine a block, you should have some Ethers in your account now.

Examining a Block

You can examine the content of a block by using the eth.getBlock() function:

```
> eth.getBlock(22)
{
  difficulty: 132352,
  extraData: "0xd98301081484676574688867f312e31312e348664617277696e",
  gasLimit: 3209750,
  gasUsed: 0,
  hash: "0xc939ead8408e911bd7fa8e4dde37b08e987c624c48f5df2379928b32de4f2021",
  logsBloom: "0x000000000000000000000000000000000000000000000000000000000000
0000000000000000000000000000000000000000000000000000000000000000000000000000000
0000000000000000000000000000000000000000000000000000000000000000000000000000000
0000000000000000000000000000000000000000000000000000000000000000000000000000000
0000000000000000000000000000000000000000000000000000000000000000000000000000000
0000000000000000000000000000000000000000000000000000000000000000000000000000000
0000000000000000000000000000000000000000000000000000000000000000000000000000000
000000000000000",
  miner: "0xe225dc6b5e85b6f2659ca310b2a17247291e6b6b",
  mixHash: "0x18ce27b4d533e1611971c20518e654d00c8d9fd86af4e50fc50537eb8f
b2e1f8",
  nonce: "0x430debc6fcf6ec20",
  number: 22,
  parentHash: "0xf74385c3e2d88b43da869b5389745b45163baa3a314961f7311a8ba8ab
b057e6",
  receiptsRoot: "0x56e81f171bcc55a6ff8345e692c0f86e5b48e01b996cadc001622fb5
e363b421",
  sha3Uncles: "0x1dcc4de8dec75d7aab85b567b6ccd41ad312451b948a7413f0a142fd40
d49347",
```

```
    size: 537,
    stateRoot: "0x9356e29a82c2b597fff48b36e1b1b39a9e57253d5c2934239d92c406b63
    589c1",
    timestamp: 1546932855,
    totalDifficulty: 3028096,
    transactions: [],
    transactionsRoot: "0x56e81f171bcc55a6ff8345e692c0f86e5b48e01b996cadc00162
    2fb5e363b421",
    uncles: []
}
```

The eth.getBlock() function takes in a number representing the block number that you want to examine. One particular interesting point to note: the miner key indicates the account that successfully mined the block.

Mining on Both Nodes

Up till this point, only **node1** is doing the mining and having all the fun (and reaping all the rewards). Why not get **node2** to do the mining too? If you try to mine on **node2** now, you will see the following error:

```
> miner.start(1)
Error: etherbase missing: etherbase must be explicitly specified
    at web3.js:3143:20
    at web3.js:6347:15
    at web3.js:5081:36
    at <anonymous>:1:1
```

Why? Simple, in order to perform mining, you need to have at least one account in your node for the rewards to be deposited into. To solve this problem, create a new account using the personal.newAccount() function. Once the account is created, you can use the miner.start() function again.

You now have two miners mining at the same time and competing for rewards. To know who is the miner of the latest block, you can use the eth.getBlock() function and checking its miner property, like this: eth.getBlock(eth.blockNumber).miner. The result would be the address of the account who managed to mine the latest block.

Transferring Ethers Between Nodes

In **node1**, let's create another account using the personal.newAccount() function. You should now have two accounts:

> **eth.accounts**

```
["0x530e822163471b0e65725cbd85dc141ff6b24d59",
"0xf439200bdfb03598e9887828399e8986447d658f"]
Let's verify how much you have in each account:
```

> **eth.getBalance(eth.accounts[0])**

```
3.376328125e+22
```

> **eth.getBalance(eth.accounts[1])**

```
0
```

To transfer some Ethers from one account to another account, you can use the eth. sendTransaction() function. But before you use it to transfer Ethers, you need to unlock the source account first, using the personal.unlockAccount() function:

> **personal.unlockAccount(eth.accounts[0])**

```
Unlock account 0x530e822163471b0e65725cbd85dc141ff6b24d59
Passphrase: <password>
```

true

```
Once the account is unlocked, you can now transfer the Ether:
```

> **eth.sendTransaction({from: eth.accounts[0], to: eth.accounts[1], value: web3.toWei(5,"ether")})**

"0xbac74dffae71c5532d83ed8ae37ff97d68dd2ab8b7f62fa2b1032f88df8d543c"

Tip   If you want to transfer Ether to another node on another computer, simply specify the address of the account you want to send to enclosed with a pair of double quotes, like this: eth.sendTransaction({from: eth.accounts[0], to: "*0x9ba6f3c9cce2b172d0a85a50101ae05f3b4c8731*", value: web3. toWei(5,"ether")})

In the preceding example, I am transferring five Ethers from the first account to the second account within the same node. The output of the function is the transaction ID. If you now check the balance of the two accounts and realize that they are still the same, then one of the following causes is likely:

- You are not currently mining. Remember, mining confirms transactions so that the transactions can be recorded on the blockchain. To resolve this, start mining on the node.

- If you are currently mining, then it is likely that the transactions have not be confirmed yet. Will a while and try to check the balance again.

After a while, you should be able to see five Ethers in the second account:

```
> eth.getBalance(eth.accounts[1])
5000000000000000000
```

Tip   If you check the balance of the first account, you are likely to see it has less than five Ethers deducted. This is because in spite of the five Ethers deducted, it is also earning rewards doing the mining. Hence, it is easier to verify the balance of the second account.

Managing Accounts

Earlier in this chapter, you learned about creating accounts in your node. I also mentioned that the account details are stored in a file with the name starting with "UTC" and saved in the ~/**MyTestNet/data/node1/keystore** directory. Let's try to dissect the content of this UTC file:

```
{
  "address": "530e822163471b0e65725cbd85dc141ff6b24d59",
  "crypto": {
    "cipher": "aes-128-ctr",
    "ciphertext": "4f817ca1925f3c54a3874e9075eb74324d6976cdc7fe1d44372457b8
    32a23987",
    "cipherparams": {
```

```
    "iv": "043fab979c36a35b53a84611e771670c"
  },
  "kdf": "scrypt",
  "kdfparams": {
    "dklen": 32,
    "n": 262144,
    "p": 1,
    "r": 8,
    "salt": "c5743e378efe354744c35e3b6cad2ae2eb1407890731fae7fc9acb085931
    c343"
  },
  "mac": "1f8e42a800824ddab06fb92c5ca8ad874f1830c39d575d4f16c4118943de8803"
  },
  "id": "00d6ad8d-96c1-4211-84ac-1d921617bd8e",
  "version": 3
}
```

The preceding shows the content of the first account in **node1** with the file name
UTC--2019-01-08T08-37-52.567662000Z--530e822163471b0e65725cbd85dc141ff6b24d59.

It contains the following:

- Your encrypted private key (encrypted using your supplied
  password).

- The public key is not stored in the JSON file as it can be derived from
  the private key.

- Your account address (which is derived from your public key). The
  account address is the last 20 bytes of the public key.

Figure 4-8 summarizes how your account address is derived.

User Account

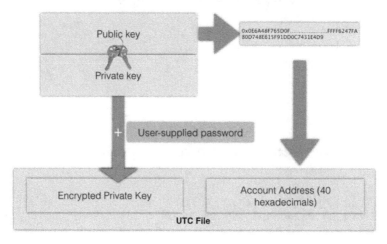

Figure 4-8. *Understanding how the accounts information is derived*

Tip   Curious about your private key? You can go to `www.myetherwallet.com/#view-wallet-info`, select the Keystore File (UTC / JSON) option, and upload your JSON UTC file. You will be asked to enter your password used to secure the account, and voila, your private key will now be displayed. Note that this is purely for educational purposes. Do not try this with your real account.

Removing Accounts

Once you use the `personal.newAccount()` function, the account is created. There is no equivalent function to remove the account. The easiest way to delete the account is to go to the ~/**MyTestNet/data/node1/keystore** directory and delete the UTC file corresponding to the account that you want to delete.

Setting the Coinbase

The `eth.coinbase` property returns the account within the node that all the mining rewards go to. In **node1**, our coinbase is our first account:

> **eth.coinbase**

"0x530e822163471b0e65725cbd85dc141ff6b24d59"

To change the coinbase, you can use the `miner.setEtherbase()` function. Let's try it now.

First, let's print out the accounts that we have in **node1**:

> **eth.accounts**

["0x530e822163471b0e65725cbd85dc141ff6b24d59",
"0xf439200bdfb03598e9887828399e8986447d658f"]
Let's change the coinbase to the second account:

> **miner.setEtherbase(eth.accounts[1])**

true

Once this is done, we can verify if the coinbase has indeed been changed to the second account:

> **eth.coinbase**

"0xf439200bdfb03598e9887828399e8986447d658f"

Summary

In this chapter, you have learned how to use Geth to create your own private Ethereum test network. You have learn how to create accounts in your node, connect to other nodes, transfer Ether between nodes, and more. Deploying your own test network is much more efficient than using one of Ethereum's test network. What's more, it allows you to experiment and have a deeper understanding of Ethereum.

## CHAPTER 5

Using the MetaMask Chrome Extension

In the previous chapter, you learned how to create your own private Ethereum test network so that you can try out the various Ethereum transactions, such as transferring Ethers to different accounts and performing mining. You also learned how to create accounts so that you can hold your own Ethers. In this chapter, you will learn how to use a Chrome extension known as the *MetaMask*. The MetaMask Chrome extension is an Ethereum wallet that allows you to hold your Ethereum account, and it will be an essential tool to help you develop and test Smart Contracts in the next few chapters.

What Is MetaMask?

MetaMask is a very useful tool that plays a pivotal role in allowing you to make your foray into the world of blockchain. Rather than attempt to define what exactly MetaMask is in one paragraph, I shall talk about the role played by MetaMask as we go along.

First and foremost, MetaMask is an Ethereum wallet. It allows you to

- Create accounts for use in the various Ethereum networks

  - It maintains the private keys for your accounts so that you can export them or import new accounts.

- Switch between the various Ethereum networks, so that your accounts can reflect the correct balance for each network

- Perform transactions between accounts

  - You can transfer Ethers from one account to another.

© Wei-Meng Lee 2019
W.-M. Lee, *Beginning Ethereum Smart Contracts Programming*,
https://doi.org/10.1007/978-1-4842-5086-0_5

- You can also hold tokens in your MetaMask accounts.

- You can also view your detail transactions on Etherscan, a blockchain explorer.

Besides being an Ethereum wallet, MetaMask also allows you to interact with the Ethereum blockchain by injecting a Javascript library called web3.js, developed by the Ethereum core team. We will discuss more on this in the next chapter when we discuss Smart Contracts.

How MetaMask Works Behind the Scene

Behind the scene, MetaMask connects to a server called INFURA (`https://infura.io/`). INFURA maintains Ethereum nodes that connect to the respective Ethereum networks. Rather than allowing INFURA to keep your private keys (which is always a security risk when your private key is kept in the cloud held by a third party), INFURA allows MetaMask to keep your private keys of your account in your local computer and simply relays the transactions to the network. Figure 5-1 shows the relationships between MetaMask, INFURA, and the Ethereum network.

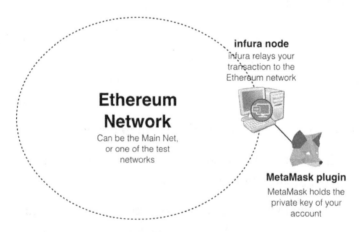

Figure 5-1. *How MetaMask works behind the scene*

When MetaMask connects to one of the Ethereum networks, it connects to one of the respective INFURA nodes:

- **Main Ethereum Network** – `https://mainnet.infura.io/metamask`

- **Ropsten Test Network** – `https://ropsten.infura.io/metamask`

- **Kovan Test Network** – `https://kovan.infura.io/metamask`

- **Rinkeby Test Network** – `https://rinkeby.infura.io/metamask`

Installing MetaMask

The easiest way to install MetaMask is to use the Chrome browser and install MetaMask as a Chrome extension. To install the MetaMask extension:

- Launch Chrome and navigate to the Chrome Web Store at `https://chrome.google.com/webstore/category/extensions`.

- Search for MetaMask.

- You should now be able to see the MetaMask extension in the search result. Click **Add to Chrome** (see Figure 5-2).

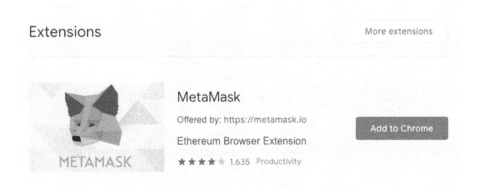

Figure 5-2. *Searching for MetaMask in the Chrome Web Store*

- You will be prompted to add MetaMask to Chrome. Click **Add extension** (see Figure 5-3).

Figure 5-3. *Adding the MetaMask extension to the Chrome browser*

- Once MetaMask is added to Chrome, you will be able to see its icon appear on the top right corner of the browser (see Figure 5-4).

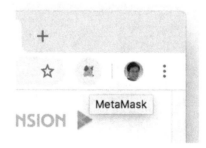

Figure 5-4. *Locating the MetaMask icon in the Chrome browser*

Signing in to MetaMask

With the MetaMask extension installed in your Chrome browser, you can now sign in to it:

- Click the MetaMask icon, and click CONTINUE (see Figure 5-5):

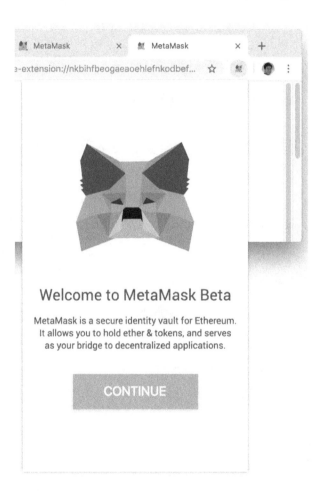

Figure 5-5. *Getting started with MetaMask*

- You will be asked to create a password for your account. Enter the password twice (see Figure 5-6) and click CREATE.

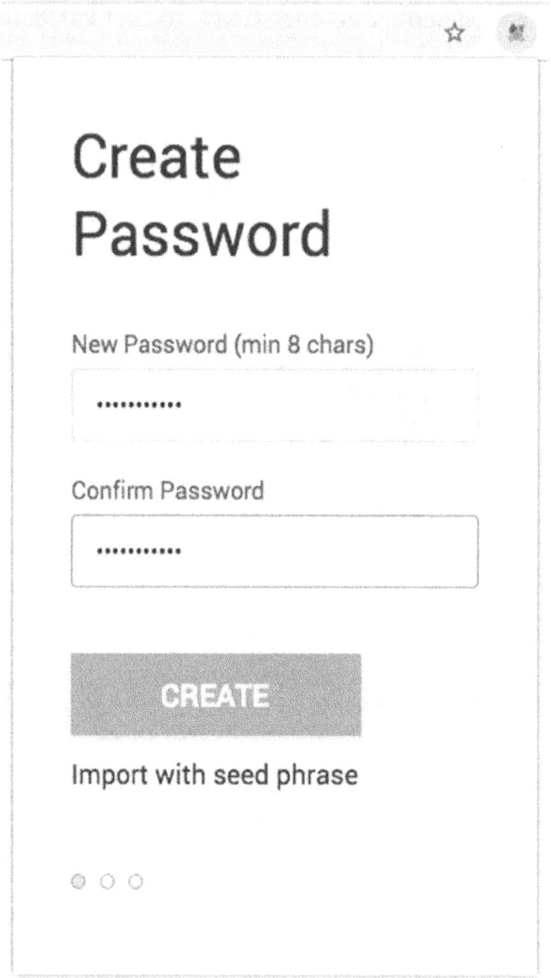

Figure 5-6. *Creating a password for MetaMask*

- In the next screen, click NEXT.

- You will be asked to agree to the Terms of Use. Scroll to the bottom of the page and click ACCEPT.

- For the next few pages, click ACCEPT a few more times.

- In the next screen, you will see your secret backup phrase. You can click the lock icon (see Figure 5-7) to reveal the 12-word secret phrase or scroll to the bottom of the page to download the 12-word secret phrase in a text file. At the bottom of the page, click NEXT.

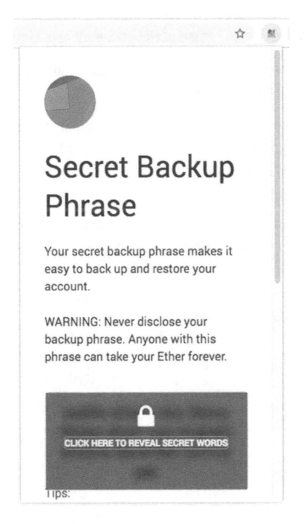

Figure 5-7. *Revealing the 12-word secret phrase*

The 12-word secret phrase allows you to recover your account in the event that you have forgotten your password. This 12-word secret phrase is known as the BIP39 (Bitcoin Improvement Proposals) *seed phrase*. MetaMask uses the BIP39 protocol to figure out how to use a set of 12-word secret phrase to get a *seed* – this seed will be used to generate a root key for each cryptocurrency (in the case of Ethereum, this is Ether).

The root key is then hashed to generate a *private key*, which will be used to generate a *public key*, which in turn will be used to generate the *public address* for an account. To generate a second account, the first private key is hashed to obtain the second private key, which is then used to generate a public key, and so on.

Using this method, the seed works with a deterministic algorithm to generate an unlimited series of addresses for your wallet.

The list of words used in the secret phrase can be found here: `https://github.com/bitcoin/bips/blob/master/bip-0039/english.txt`. It is based on a list of 2048 words, with 12 words selected in a particular order.

- In the next screen, you will be asked to select the 12 words in the specific order that it was shown. This is to confirm that you have the correct phrase.

- You can now view your account or buy Ether from Coinbase. For now, click the VIEW ACCOUNT button (see Figure 5-8).

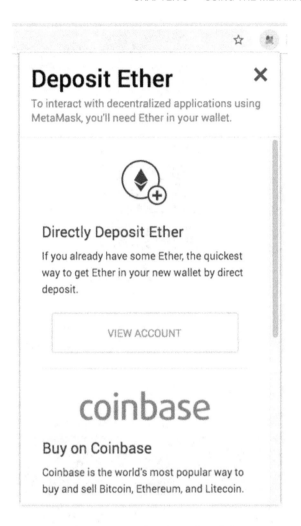

Figure 5-8. *You are now ready to view the details of the account*

- You should now see your account information as shown in Figure 5-9. Your account information is also displayed as a QR code, and you can also view your account details on Etherscan or export your private key (so that you can import your account into another computer). For now, close the pop-up by clicking "X".

Figure 5-9. *Your account address is also shown in QR code*

- Your account should now see a balance of 0 ETH (see Figure 5-10).

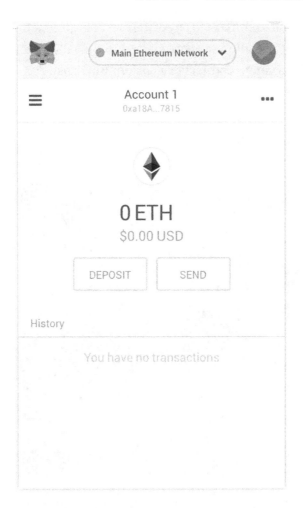

Figure 5-10. *Current balance of your account*

Selecting Ethereum Networks

By default, MetaMask is connected to the Main Ethereum Network. This is the real network where real Ethers are used for transactions, running Smart Contracts, and so on. For development purposes, you would not want to connect to the real network; rather you should connect to one of the test networks available:

- Ropsten Test Network

- Kovan Test Network

- Rinkeby Test Network

MetaMask allows you to connect to any of the preceding test networks (see Figure 5-11). In addition, MetaMask also allows you to connect to a local Ethereum node listening at port 8545. It also allows you to connect to a custom RPC host.

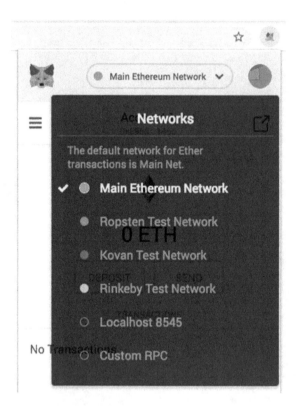

Figure 5-11. *Selecting the Ethereum network to connect to*

For this chapter, we shall use the Ropsten Test Network. So, make sure you select the Ropsten Test Network in MetaMask.

Getting Ethers

Once you are connected to the Ropsten Test Network, the first thing to do would be to get some free Ethers so that you can use it to pay for transacting on the network.

To get free Ethers:

- Click the DEPOSIT button (see Figure 5-12).

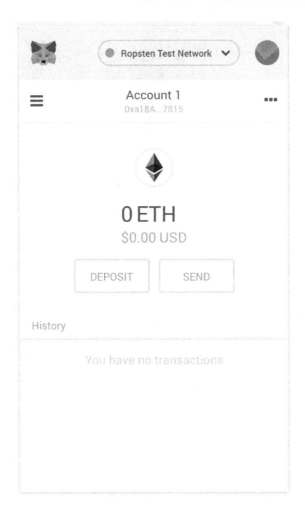

Figure 5-12.   *Get free Ethers for your account using the DEPOSIT button*

- Scroll to the bottom of the page and click GET ETHER (see Figure 5-13).

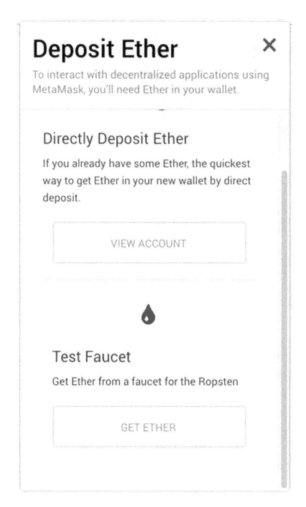

Figure 5-13. *Click the GET ETHER button to get free Ethers from the test faucet*

- This will bring you to the MetaMask Ether Faucet page (see Figure 5-14). Click the "request 1 ether from faucet" button.

Figure 5-14. *Getting free Ethers from the test faucet*

- In MetaMask, you will now see that the Test Ether Faucet would like to connect to your account (see Figure 5-15). Click CONNECT.

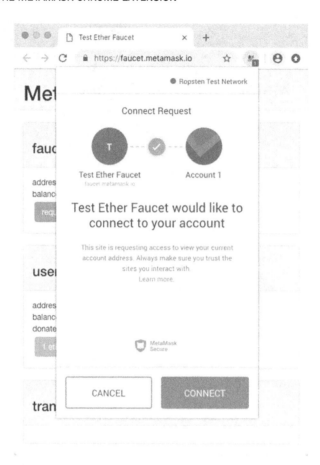

Figure 5-15. *You need to connect the Test Ether Faucet to your account before your free Ether can be credited into your account*

- At the bottom of the MetaMask Ether Faucet page, you will now see a transaction hyperlink (see Figure 5-16). Clicking on it allows you to see the status of the transaction on Etherscan (see Figure 5-17).

Figure 5-16. *The link to the transaction on Etherscan*

Etherscan is an Ethereum Blockchain Explorer. It allows you to search the blockchain for transactions, addresses, tokens, prices, as well as activities happening on the blockchain.

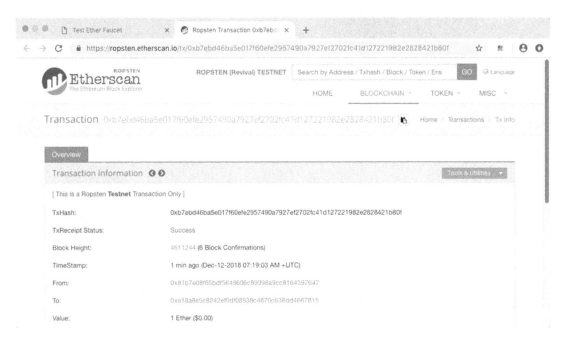

Figure 5-17. *Viewing the transaction on Etherscan*

- After a while, you should be able to see one token deposited into your account (see Figure 5-18).

You can request for more Ethers by clicking the "request 1 ether from faucet" button on the MetaMask Ether Faucet page multiple times. Each button that you clicked will earn you one free Ether. However, do note that sometimes if you click the button too many times, it will respond with an error message that says "User is greedy." So don't be greedy!

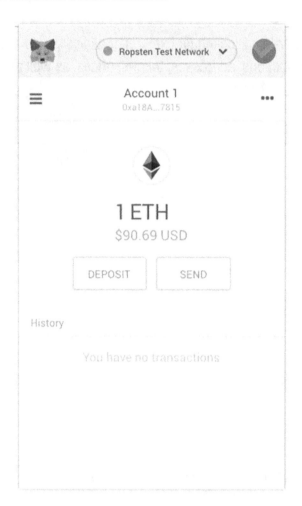

Figure 5-18. *The free 1 Ether credited into your account*

All Ethers in the test networks have no monetary value. So, don't be too excited if you see the US dollars equivalent of your Ether balance displayed in MetaMask.

It is important to remember that the amount of Ether you have in your account is valid only for the particular Ethereum network that you have obtained it from. For example, if you now switch to another test network, say the Rinkeby Test Network, your account balance would be reset to 0.

Creating Additional Accounts

MetaMask allows you to create multiple accounts. This is useful when you want to learn how to transfer Ethers from one account to another. It is also useful when testing and debugging your Smart Contracts.

To create additional accounts in MetaMask:

- Click the colored icon located at the top right corner of MetaMask (see Figure 5-19).

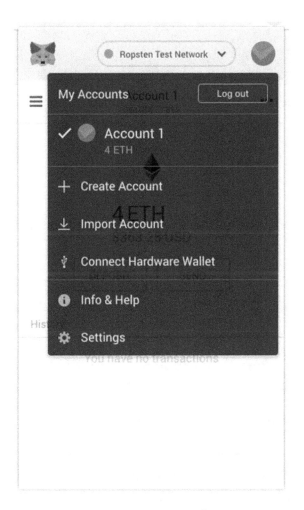

Figure 5-19. *Creating new accounts in MetaMask*

- Click the Create Account item.

- In the NEW ACCOUNT screen, click CREATE.

- You can now see the new account created (Account 2, see Figure 5-20).

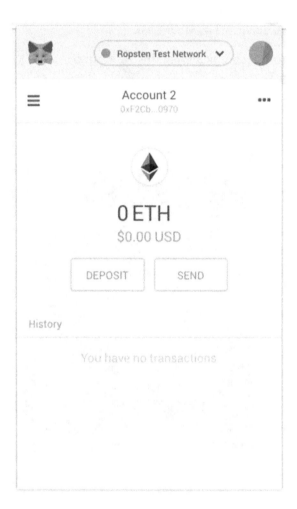

Figure 5-20. *The second newly created account*

You can create as many accounts as you want. In fact, for testing your Smart Contracts, you should create at least three accounts for testing purposes.

- To switch between accounts, click the colored icon (see Figure 5-21) and select the account you want to switch to.

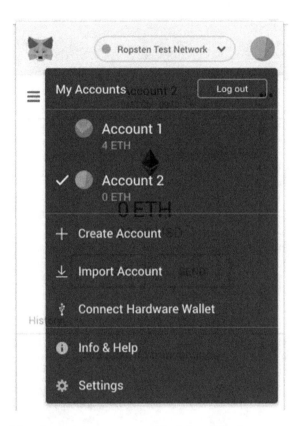

Figure 5-21. *Switching between accounts in MetaMask*

Transferring Ethers

MetaMask allows you to transfer Ethers from one account to another very easily. You can transfer to another account within MetaMask or an external account using its public address.

To transfer Ether from one account to another

- Switch to Account 1.

- Click the SEND button.

- You will now see the screen shown in Figure 5-22.

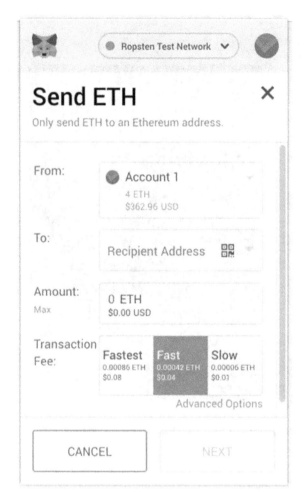

Figure 5-22. *Sending Ethers to another account*

- To send Ether to another local account, click the down arrow at the
  To: item (see Figure 5-23). Select Account 2 in this example.

Figure 5-23. *Selecting which account to send the Ether to*

To send Ether to an external account, click the QR code icon, and you will be able to use your Webcam to scan the QR code of the public address of the external account.

- Specify how many Ethers you want to send (one in this example), and select the fast transaction fee (see Figure 5-24). Click NEXT.

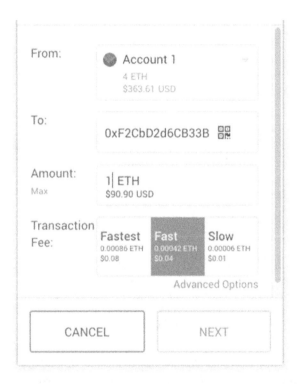

Figure 5-24. *Specifying how many Ethers to send and selecting the transaction fee*

In general, the higher the transaction fee, the faster the transaction will be processed.

- You will now see the total amount that you will incur for this transaction (see Figure 5-25). Click CONFIRM.

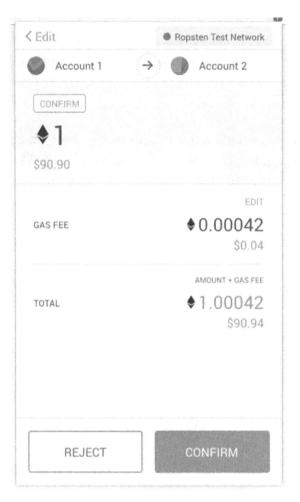

Figure 5-25. *Confirming the transaction*

The total transaction amount is the amount of Ether you are transferring, plus the transaction fee. The transaction fee is also known as the *gas fee*.

- When the transaction goes through, your account should be deducted by the total transaction amount (see Figure 5-26).

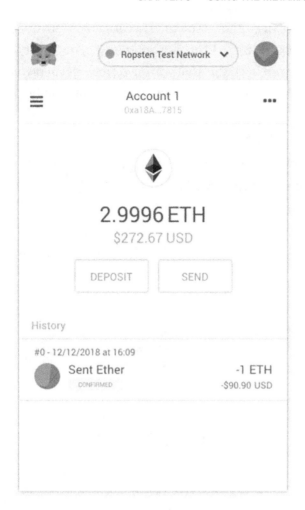

Figure 5-26. *Your account balance after the transfer*

- You can verify that the Ether has been transferred to Account 2 by switching to Account 2.

Recovering Accounts

MetaMask has an inbuilt system that allows you to recover your accounts safely and securely. There are a few possible scenarios where you would need to recover your accounts:

- You have forgotten your password to login to MetaMask.

- You need to transfer your account from one computer to another (perhaps you have bought a new computer or lost your old one).

In either case, MetaMask allows you to very easily recover your existing accounts provided you have backed up the 12-word pass phrase. The beauty of using the 12-word pass phrase is that all your accounts that you have created can be recovered. Say you have created three accounts in MetaMask, all the accounts can be recovered as long as you have the 12-word pass phrase.

To recover your accounts:

- Click the "Import using account seed phrase" link in the MetaMask login screen (see Figure 5-27).

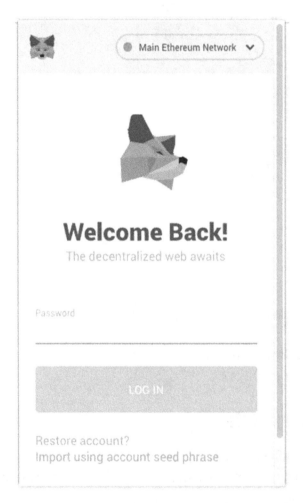

Figure 5-27. *Recovering your account(s) using the 12-word secret seed phrase*

- You will now be redirected to a web page that shows the same login page. Again, click the "Import using account seed phrase" link.

- Enter the 12-word seed phrase in the exact order that it was provided to you earlier (see Figure 5-28). You also need to assign a new password to protect your account. Click RESTORE.

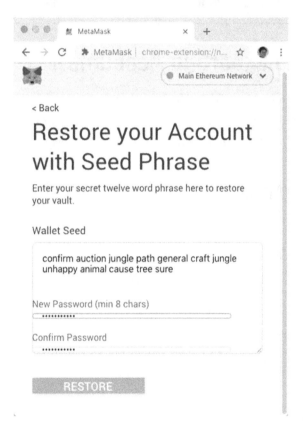

Figure 5-28. *Restoring your accounts and resetting your password*

- You will now find your original Account 1. However, the other accounts that you have also created earlier is not visible.

You should see the Account 1 with the same amount of Ether that you had earlier.

- Go ahead and create a new account like you have done so earlier. You will now see your Account 2. In fact, all the original accounts can be recovered this way, and the amount of Ether that you had earlier will automatically be recovered.

Your Account 2 should also have the same amount of Ether that you had earlier.

Importing and Exporting Accounts

You can export your accounts in MetaMask so that they can be imported on another computer. All you need to do is to export the private key of your account and import it in another computer using the same private key

Exporting Accounts

To export an account:

- Select the account that you want to export.

- Select the ... displayed on the right of the account name, and select Account Details (see Figure 5-29).

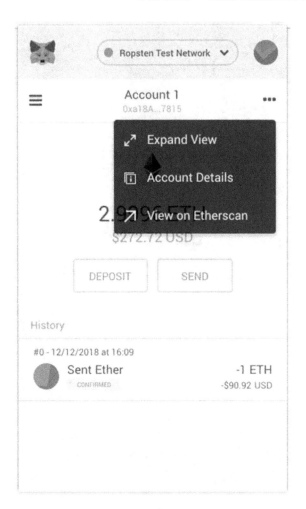

Figure 5-29. *Viewing your account details*

- Click the EXPORT PRIVATE KEY button (see Figure 5-30).

Figure 5-30. *Exporting the private key for your account*

- Enter your MetaMask password and click CONFIRM (see Figure 5-31).

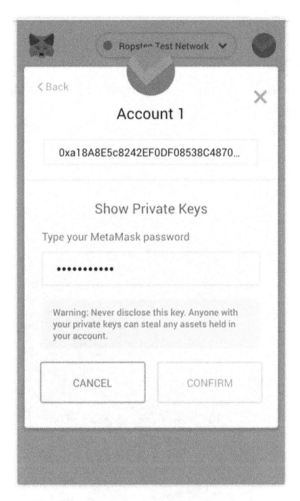

Figure 5-31. *Viewing the private key for your account*

- You should now see your private key. Click it to copy it into the
  clipboard and save it securely to a text file.

When dealing with accounts in the Main Ethereum Network, do be very cautious
when exporting your private key and be sure to save it in a secure location. Once
the private key is leaked, the assets in your accounts can be stolen easily. Of
course, when dealing with one of the test networks, it is far less important as the
assets in the test networks have no monetary value.

Importing Accounts

To import an account into MetaMask:

- Click the colored icon located at the top right corner of MetaMask (see Figure 5-32). Click Import Account.

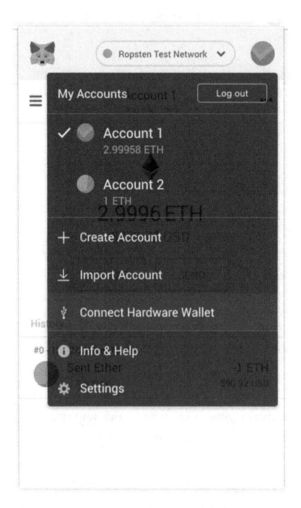

Figure 5-32. *Importing an existing account*

- Paste the private key into the text box as shown in Figure 5-33. Click IMPORT. The account would now be imported into MetaMask.

You can only import a new account based on a private key that is not already in your MetaMask. If not, the import will not be successful. Also, for accounts that you have imported, they are not recoverable using the 12-word secret phrase. To restore these accounts, you have to use their private key or JSON file.

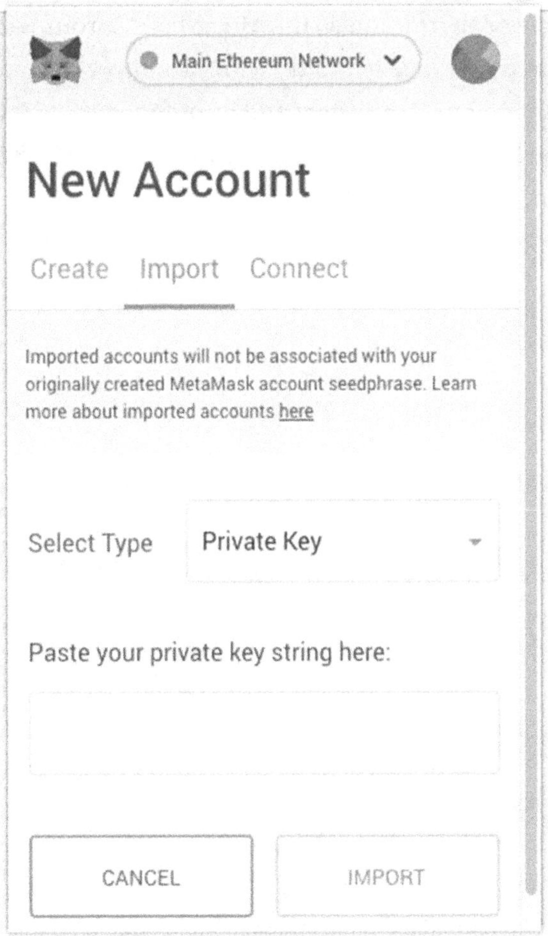

Figure 5-33. *Pasting the private key to import the account*

There are two ways to import accounts into MetaMask – using private key or JSON File. In Chapter 4, you learned about the accounts stored in the JSON files. This is what you can use to import the accounts in Geth into the MetaMask.

Summary

In this chapter, you have seen how to use the MetaMask Chrome extension to manage your Ethereum accounts. You have learned the basics – how to create accounts, transfer Ethers between accounts, as well as export and import accounts into MetaMask. In the following chapters, you have more opportunities to see MetaMask in action and how it helps you to run dApps in your web browsers.

CHAPTER 6

Getting Started with Smart Contract

So far you have learned how to create your private test Ethereum network. You have also learned how to manage your Ethers using the MetaMask Chrome extension. In this chapter, you will learn about one of the most interesting and exciting features of Ethereum – Smart Contract. You will have a quick look at how a Smart Contract looks like as well as how to test it. In the next few chapters, we will dive into the details of Smart Contracts.

Your First Smart Contract

You are now ready to write your first Smart Contract. To do that, you can use any of your favorite code editors, such as Visual Studio Code or even vi.

Tip Visual Studio Code has several solidity extensions that you can install to make the writing of Smart Contracts easy.

My personal favorite is the **Remix IDE**. The Remix IDE is a suite of tools to interact with the Ethereum blockchain. It can compile your Smart Contract into bytecode, generate the ABI (application binary interface), as well as deploy your contracts into the various Ethereum test networks (as well as the real Ethereum blockchain). The ability to compile the contract on-the-fly makes it a very handy tool to learn Smart Contracts programming. Hence, I strongly recommend that you use it to write your contracts.

For this book, we shall use the Remix IDE for writing Smart Contracts.

127

© Wei-Meng Lee 2019
W.-M. Lee, *Beginning Ethereum Smart Contracts Programming*,
https://doi.org/10.1007/978-1-4842-5086-0_6

Note   To compile a Solidity Smart Contract, you need to use the **solc** compiler. But if you use Remix IDE, you don't have to explicitly use it to compile your contract.

Using the Remix IDE

To use the Remix IDE, launch the Chrome browser and load the following URL: https://remix.ethereum.org/. If you are loading the Remix IDE the first time, you will see a sample contract called ballot.sol as shown in Figure 6-1. This is a sample contract that you can look at if you want to know how Solidity works.

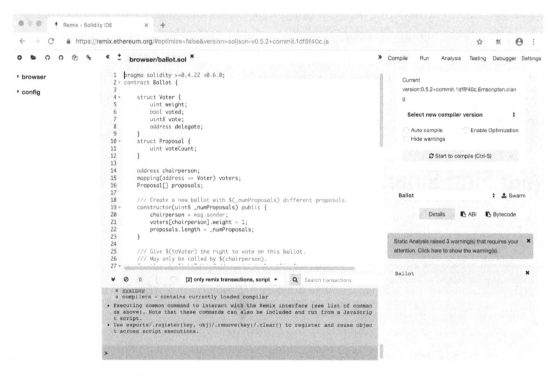

Figure 6-1. *Using the Remix IDE to create your Smart Contract*

For now, you can just ignore the ballot.sol contract.

Tip   All contracts created using the Remix IDE is stored locally in your browser cache.

To create a new contract, click the + icon located at the top left corner of Remix IDE. Once you clicked that, you will be asked to give a new name to your contract. Name it as Calculator.sol (see Figure 6-2) and click OK.

Caution   You might want to close the current script before clicking the "+" icon.

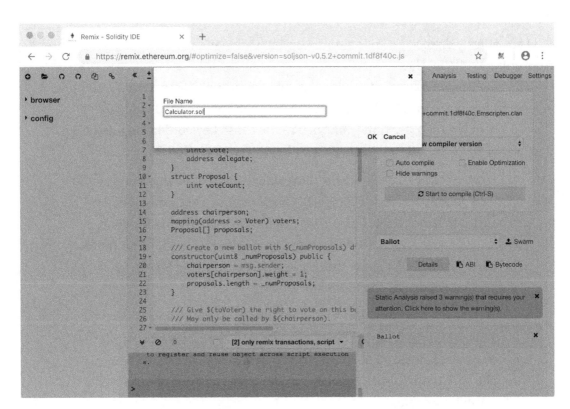

Figure 6-2. *Creating and naming your new Smart Contract in the Remix IDE*

Let's now create a simple contract named Calculator. Populate the Remix IDE with the following:

```
pragma solidity ^0.5.2;

contract Calculator {
  function arithmetics(uint num1, uint num2) public
    pure returns (uint sum, uint product) {
    sum = num1 + num2;
```

```
    product = num1 * num2;
  }
  function multiply(uint num1, uint num2) public
    pure returns (uint) {
    return num1 * num2;
  }
}
```

Let's quickly dissect the code and see how it works, and then we can run it and see the result.

First, the `pragma` statement means that the contract will compile with a compiler version beginning with 0.5.2; but it will not work with version 0.6.0 or higher.

Next, the `contract` keyword (think of it as the `class` keyword in languages like C# and Java) defines the contract named `Calculator`. It contains two functions:

- `arithmetics` – This function takes in two arguments – `num1` and `num2`, of type `uint` (unsigned integer). It has a `public` access modifier, and it returns a tuple containing two members – `sum` and `product`, each of type `uint`. The two statements within the function computes the sum and products of the two arguments, and their values are automatically returned from the function.

- `multiply` – This function is similar to the preceding function, except that the return statement is a little different. Here, I specify that I want to return a single value of type `uint`, but I do not specify the name of the variable to return. Instead, I use the `return` keyword to return the specific variable.

Notice that both functions have the `pure` keyword in its declaration. The `pure` keyword indicates that the function will not access nor change the value of state variables. The use of this keyword is important – as no modification is made to the blockchain, values can be returned without network verifications. As such, it is also free to call this function without needing any gas.

Note   State variables are storage on the blockchain used to store values, such as the variables you declare in your contract. We will discuss more about state variables in the next chapter.

Compiling the Contract

The Remix IDE allows you to automatically compile the code as you type. To enable this, select the **Compile** tab on the right side of the screen and check the **Auto compile** option, as shown in Figure 6-3. If there are any warnings, you will see them in a blue box. Here, our code has two warnings.

Figure 6-3. *The Remix IDE automatically compiles your code as you type*

Clicking on the warning will bring you to the **Analysis** tab (see Figure 6-4). For our case, the compile is warning me that my variables have similar names. That's alright, for now.

Figure 6-4. *Viewing the warnings for your code*

If there is a syntax error, then an error will appear under the **Compile** tab (see Figure 6-5). Clicking on the error will bring you to the code. In this example, a statement is missing a semicolon (;) at the end of the line, so that can be fixed easily.

Figure 6-5. *Viewing rhe syntax error of your code*

Testing the Smart Contract Using the JavaScript VM

Once the code is compiled and error free, you can test it directly within Remix IDE. Click the **Run** tab. Click the drop-down list next to the **Environment** option and you should be able to see three options (see Figure 6-6):

- **JavaScript VM** – Simulates running your Smart Contract locally without actually deploying it onto the blockchain.

- **Injected Web3** – Uses a plugin such as MetaMask in your web browser to inject a **web3** object (see Chapter 9 for more information) so that your Smart Contract can be associated with an account.

- **Web3 Provider** – Connects directly to an Ethereum node so that your Smart Contract can be associated with an account. Requires you to run an Ethereum node such as **geth**.

Figure 6-6. *The JavaScript VM allows you to test your code directly*

Select the JavaScript VM so that you can test the contract without deploying it to a blockchain.

Next, click the **Deploy** button (see Figure 6-7). You should now see your contract under the **Deployed Contracts** section.

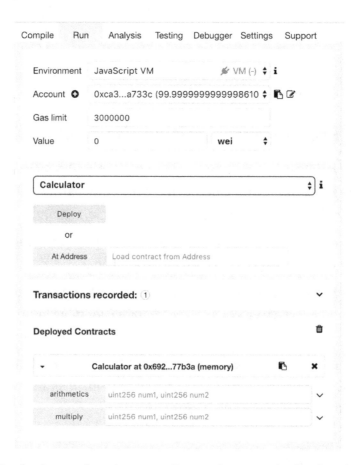

Figure 6-7. *Deploying and testing your Smart Contract in the Remix IDE*

Click the arrow icons displayed to the left of the Calculator contract to reveal the two functions in your contract, each displayed in a blue colored box.

Enter the text as shown in Figure 6-8 and click the **arithmetics** button. The result will now be displayed underneath it.

Figure 6-8. *Testing the first function in the Smart Contract*

Tip   The color of the button serves a purpose – blue-colored button means that it is free to call the function. Red-colored button, on the other hand, means that you need to incur gas to call it. We have a chance to see red-color button in the next chapter.

Enter the numbers for the next button and then click on it (Figure 6-9). You will see its output.

1: uint256: product 30

| multiply | 7,8 | ⌄ |

0: uint256: 56

Figure 6-9. *Testing the second function in the Smart Contract*

Getting the ABI and Bytecode of the Contract

Now that the contract has been tested to work correctly, it is time to test it on a real blockchain. But before you do it, there is something else you need to understand. When a contract is compiled, there are two items of interest:

- ABI (application binary interface) – The ABI is a JSON string that describes the makeup of the contract – the functions as well as the parameter types of each function.

- Bytecode – When a contract is compiled, it is compiled into opcodes (think of opcode as the assembly language for your computer). Each opcode has its hexadecimal counterparts. The bytecode is basically a collection of each opcode's hexadecimal representation.

In the **Compile** tab, you will be able to see two icons representing ABI and Bytecode (see Figure 6-10). If you click the ABI icon, the ABI will be copied to the clipboard.

Figure 6-10. *The ABI and Bytecode buttons provide easy access to the ABI and bytecode of the contract*

The ABI looks like the following:

```
[
  {
    "constant": true,
    "inputs": [
      {
        "name": "num1",
        "type": "uint256"
      },
      {
        "name": "num2",
```

```
          "type": "uint256"
      }
    ],
    "name": "multiply",
    "outputs": [
      {
        "name": "",
        "type": "uint256"
      }
    ],
    "payable": false,
    "stateMutability": "pure",
    "type": "function"
  },
  {
    "constant": true,
    "inputs": [
      {
        "name": "num1",
        "type": "uint256"
      },
      {
        "name": "num2",
        "type": "uint256"
      }
    ],
    "name": "arithmetics",
    "outputs": [
      {
        "name": "sum",
        "type": "uint256"
      },
      {
        "name": "product",
        "type": "uint256"
```

```
    }
  ],
  "payable": false,
  "stateMutability": "pure",
  "type": "function"
  }
]
```

For the byte code, you can click the bytecode icon, and similarly, the bytecode (along with the opcode and other details) will be copied to the clipboard. However, personally, I would like to obtain the bytecode by clicking the **Details** button. A pop-up window will now appear. Scroll down the list and look for the section labeled BYTECODE (see Figure 6-11). The bytecode you need is the one highlighted in the figure (the value of the "object" key).

```
BYTECODE 🗎 ❷

{
    "linkReferences": {},
    "object": "60806040523480156100105760000080fd5b506101448061002
    "opcodes": "PUSH1 0x80 PUSH1 0x40 MSTORE CALLVALUE DUP1 ISZE
    "sourceMap": "27:302:0:-;;;;8:9:-1;5:2;;;30:1;27;20:12;5:2;2
}
```

Figure 6-11. *Locating the bytecode of the contract through the Details button*

For your reference, the bytecode looks like this:

60806040523480156100105760000080fd5b506101448061002060003960000f3fe60806040523
480156100105760000080fd5b5060043610610053576000357c01000000000000000000000000
000000000000000000000000000000000090048063165c4a161461006058578063 8c12d8f014610
0a4575b600080fd5b61008e60048036036040811015611006e57600080fd5b81019080803590
6020019092919080359060200190929190505050506100f7565b60405180828152602001915
060405180910390f35b6100da60048036036040811015 6100ba57600080fd5b81019080803590
6020019092919080359060200190929190505050610104565b604051808381526020018281828

15260200192505050604051809103906f35b6000818302905092915050565b60008082840191
5082840290509250929050566fea165627a7a72305820b9f9a0327fd83c277fb8803cb261ca4
c887d5b961499230c7e454dda5f06f6720029

Loading the Smart Contract onto Geth

In Chapter 4, you learned how to create your own private Ethereum test network using
the Geth client. Let's now load the Calculator Smart Contract onto the test network and
see how it can be called and used.

First, create two text files named **Calculator.abi** and **Calculator.bin** and save them
in the ~/**MyTestNet/** folder. Populate the **Calculator.abi** file with the following:

```
var CalculatorContract = eth.contract([ { "constant": true,
"inputs": [ { "name": "num1", "type": "uint256" }, { "name": "num2",
"type": "uint256" } ], "name": "multiply", "outputs": [ { "name": "",
"type": "uint256" } ], "payable": false, "stateMutability": "pure",
"type": "function" }, { "constant": true, "inputs": [ { "name": "num1",
"type": "uint256" }, { "name": "num2", "type": "uint256" } ],
"name": "arithmetics", "outputs": [ { "name": "sum", "type": "uint256" },
{ "name": "product", "type": "uint256" } ], "payable": false,
"stateMutability": "pure", "type": "function" } ])
```

Basically, the **Calculator.abi** file contains a JavaScript statement that defines the
Smart Contract named `CalculatorContract` using its ABI. Observe that earlier on
when you extracted the ABI of the contract from the Remix IDE, it was formatted in
multiple lines. In the preceding example, you need to condense the multilines ABI into
a single line.

Tip   How do you convert a multiline JSON text into a single-line text? Easy. Paste
the multiline JSON text into the address bar of the Chrome browser. Then, select it
again and copy and paste it into the Calculator.abi file. Voila!

Next, populate the **Calculator.bin** file with the following:

```
personal.unlockAccount(eth.accounts[0])
var calculator = CalculatorContract.new(
    { from: eth.accounts[0],
data:"0x60806040523480156100105760008 0fd5b50610144806100206000396000f3fe608
06040523480156100105760008 0fd5b5060043610610053576000357c010000000000000000
000000000000000000000000000000000000000090048063165c4a16146100585780638c12d
8f0146100a4575b600080fd5b61008e60048036036040811015610 06e57600080fd5b810190
8080359060200190929190803590602001909291905050506100f7565b60405180828152602
00191505060405180910390f35b6100da600480360360408110156100ba57600080fd5b8101
9080803590602001909291908035906020019092919050505 0610104565b604051808381526
020018281526020019250505060405180910390f35b60008183029050929150506 5b600080
828401915082840290509250925092905056fea165627a7a72305820b9f9a0327fd83c277fb8803
cb261ca4c887d5b961499230c7e454dda5f06f6720029"
,gas:500000 })
```

The preceding first unlocks the first account in the node and then loads the Smart Contract using its bytecode. Essentially, you are deploying the Smart Contract onto the blockchain. Deploying a Smart Contract onto the blockchain requires Ether, and hence you need to specify the maximum amount of gas to be used, as well as unlock the account to use for the deployment.

Now that you have prepared the code to load the Smart Contract onto the private test network, let's now spin up the nodes that make up the private test network.

Note   In Chapter 4, you learned how to create three nodes – **node1**, **node2**, and **node3**. For now, we are going to spin up **node2** first.

In Terminal, type the following command to spin up **node2**:

```
$ geth --datadir ~/MyTestNet/data/node2 --port 30304 --nodiscover
--networkid 2345 console 2>console2.log
```

In the Geth JavaScript Console for **node2**, type the following command:

```
> loadScript("Calculator.abi")
true
```

This will load the definition of the Smart Contract named `CalculatorContract`. Next, type in the following command:

```
> loadScript("Calculator.bin")
Unlock account 0xdf86b352fa089f7a047cb0928ca4b70bb8e2f753
Passphrase: <password>
true
```

You need to unlock your account as you are going to deploy the contract. Next, type the following command:

```
> calculator
{
  abi: [{
      constant: true,
      inputs: [{...}, {...}],
      name: "multiply",
      outputs: [{...}],
      payable: false,
      stateMutability: "pure",
      type: "function"
  }, {
      constant: true,
      inputs: [{...}, {...}],
      name: "arithmetics",
      outputs: [{...}, {...}],
      payable: false,
      stateMutability: "pure",
      type: "function"
  }],
  address: undefined,
  transactionHash: "0xd1a680e5ba4ee45bee75dcdaf20c28037cdc7399981909e02dac1
  a59bce0abe9"
}
```

Type the following command:

```
> calculator.multiply
undefined
```

You get **undefined** because the contract has not been deployed yet. To do so, you need to start mining:

```
> miner.start(1)
null
```

After a while when the block containing the Smart Contract has been mined, you can try the command again:

```
> calculator.multiply
function()
```

If you see the preceding output, the contract is now deployed onto the blockchain. If not, wait a while for the mining to complete. It may take a while for the mining to complete, so you need to be patient.

Testing the Contract

Once a contract is deployed, it is officially added to the blockchain (in this case it is the private test network), and anyone with its contract address and ABI can interact with it. Type the following command to get the address of the Smart Contract:

```
> calculator.address
"0xfaa3aa5387da108ed7070d6dbae97a8cd630d3dd"
```

You can also examine the ABI of the contract:

```
> calculator.abi
[{
    constant: true,
    inputs: [{
        name: "num1",
        type: "uint256"
    }, {
        name: "num2",
        type: "uint256"
    }],
```

```
    name: "multiply",
    outputs: [{
        name: "",
        type: "uint256"
    }],
    payable: false,
    stateMutability: "pure",
    type: "function"
}, {
    constant: true,
    inputs: [{
        name: "num1",
        type: "uint256"
    }, {
        name: "num2",
        type: "uint256"
    }],
    name: "arithmetics",
    outputs: [{
        name: "sum",
        type: "uint256"
    }, {
        name: "product",
        type: "uint256"
    }],
    payable: false,
    stateMutability: "pure",
    type: "function"
}]
```

Tip   The preceding command returns the address and ABI of the contract. To call the contract from another node, you just need the address and ABI of the contract

---

Let's now try out the contract to see if it works as expected. Type the following commands:

```
> calculator.multiply.call(7,8)
56
> calculator.arithmetics.call(3,4)
[7, 12]
```

If you see the preceding outputs, this means that the Smart Contract is loaded and running correctly.

Calling the Contract from Another Node

Now that the Smart Contract is loaded and deployed in **node2**, let's try to call the contract from another node. Let's start **node1** using the following command:

```
$ geth --datadir ~/MyTestNet/data/node1 --networkid 2345 console
2>console1.log
```

Before proceeding with the following steps, be sure that **node2** is paired and synchronized with **node1**, so that both have the same blockchain. Chapter 4 discussed how to pair them up using the admin.addPeer() function.

Note   Go ahead and pair the **node1** with **node2** before continuing.

Once the nodes are paired, type the following command in **node1**:

```
> var calculator = eth.contract([ { "constant": true,
"inputs": [ { "name": "num1", "type": "uint256" }, { "name": "num2",
"type": "uint256" } ], "name": "multiply", "outputs": [ { "name": "",
"type": "uint256" } ], "payable": false, "stateMutability": "pure",
"type": "function" }, { "constant": true, "inputs": [ { "name": "num1",
"type": "uint256" }, { "name": "num2", "type": "uint256" } ],
"name": "arithmetics", "outputs": [ { "name": "sum", "type": "uint256" },
{ "name": "product", "type": "uint256" } ], "payable": false,
"stateMutability": "pure", "type": "function" }
]).at("0xfaa3aa5387da108ed7070d6dbae97a8cd630d3dd")
```

Tip   Replace *0xfaa3aa5387da108ed7070d6dbae97a8cd630d3dd* with the actual address of your contract.

The preceding command loads the contract using the Smart Contract's ABI and its address. The `eth.contract()` function takes in the two arguments in the following format: `eth.contract(<contract_abi>).at(<contract_address>)`.

Next, type the following command:

```
> calculator
{
  abi: [{
      constant: true,
      inputs: [{...}, {...}],
      name: "multiply",
      outputs: [{...}],
      payable: false,
      stateMutability: "pure",
      type: "function"
  }, {
      constant: true,
      inputs: [{...}, {...}],
      name: "arithmetics",
      outputs: [{...}, {...}],
      payable: false,
      stateMutability: "pure",
      type: "function"
  }],
  address: "0xfaa3aa5387da108ed7070d6dbae97a8cd630d3dd",
  transactionHash: null,
  allEvents: function(),
  arithmetics: function(),
  multiply: function()
}
```

The preceding output shows that the contract has been loaded successfully from the blockchain. To test if it works, try the following command:

```
> calculator.multiply.call(7,8)
56
> calculator.arithmetics.call(3,4)
[7, 12]
```

Summary

In this chapter, you had a quick look at how a Smart Contract looks like and how it works. In the next few chapter, we will dive into the details of a Smart Contract and the various ways you can interact with it.

## CHAPTER 7

Testing Smart Contracts Using Ganache

In Chapter 4, you learned how to create your own private test Ethereum network using the Ethereum client – *Geth*. While Geth is not that difficult to use to set up an Ethereum blockchain, it still takes considerable effort to set one up. In addition, you also need to create accounts and perform mining in order to obtain Ethers so that you can use them to deploy Smart Contracts and for performing transactions.

A much better option is to use a tool that can emulate an Ethereum blockchain, together with all the required accounts so that you can just focus on testing your Smart Contracts. Well, such tool does exist, and it is called – *Ganache*.

Ganache is a personal Ethereum blockchain that allows you to test and deploy your Smart Contracts without needing to connect to a real blockchain or set up your own blockchain using an Ethereum client like Geth.

Tip   Ganache was previous known as TestRPC.

In this chapter, you will learn how to download and install Ganache and how to test and deploy your Smart Contracts onto Ganache.

Downloading and Installing Ganache

Ganache comes in two flavors – as a desktop GUI app and as a command line tool. They are both available on the Windows, Mac, and Linux platforms. In the following sections, you will learn how to install the desktop as well as the command-line version of Ganache.

© Wei-Meng Lee 2019
W.-M. Lee, *Beginning Ethereum Smart Contracts Programming*,
https://doi.org/10.1007/978-1-4842-5086-0_7

Command-Line Interface

The command-line version of Ganache is a Node.js-based Ethereum client. It uses *EthereumJS* library to simulate full client behavior and make developing Ethereum applications much faster. It also includes all popular RPC functions and features (like events) and can be run deterministically to make development a breeze.

To install command-line version of Ganache, you would need to install Node.js on your computer. You can then use **npm** to install the tool.

In Terminal (or Command Prompt), type the following command to install the Ganache command-line interface (CLI):

```
$ npm install -g ganache-cli
```

Once the Ganache CLI is installed, you can launch Ganache using the following command:

```
$ ganache-cli
```

You will see the following:

```
Ganache CLI v6.3.0 (ganache-core: 2.4.0)


Available Accounts
==================
(0) 0xce2a65ca22188ac0f4efe35f5936f3c0dc530246 (~100 ETH)
(1) 0x7dd09408274683cf2968034f1a64846069ea2e0f (~100 ETH)
(2) 0xdb8c5742be2a5ded84cdd742335f5224b77d847d (~100 ETH)
(3) 0x76270d1ea676939ab6ea29dcb4d9320b6855ff0d (~100 ETH)
(4) 0xf3183fb25c7305689de42ae603993eb9bfc410d7 (~100 ETH)
(5) 0x2b0b625aaa7b7474567223179f17899d5b28257a (~100 ETH)
(6) 0x947f22c0de05ce218e5f80c116fd94a0bc379896 (~100 ETH)
(7) 0x5fd0f170ca98bf45e1f04256a544ade5a31952b0 (~100 ETH)
(8) 0xb3326cfa9180f7f54ebfbec433027a52e672d3b2 (~100 ETH)
(9) 0x0f36e01ce6b6db257c55d5ffe2d13690734a6c77 (~100 ETH)
```

Private Keys
==================

(0) 0xb822773982826eb87481f50ac4a3a6df8e3ff533a64b2c0a67604666e51f18cc
(1) 0x81db3467f2827785aa82b2374de46ad82468c4ef97b3dbafcb7421be78351032
(2) 0x4a5a3ef65431fa3ea41a21ed6fcebf9f8105ea4415b1c155b2fe9568105b93f1
(3) 0xffc74b45809c25c5c4fcd6ef3a80e2259a6eddda1c0cb03bd94f47a57e04e897
(4) 0x48481c042b93f74adb353ba5439e7071d0903922f0f4b7917412e4cf2354cf4e
(5) 0xc3952aba303a774ebfe646918ae6a263974abfdc9a6979bab32d47c211cb770b
(6) 0xe920e8da927b72705879c2f52d95a97d4cc4a7d1a9280e5484dc0a4cd713694f
(7) 0x6c9b8d4a7399320f81f7aa773084b498a15fdfc754004a802814ba33b41386c1
(8) 0x84a6415c523e4b140218232597bf93081c225f5e041ee88ca7145f456a873748
(9) 0x8c93dd96ae7e58e9bfe8d399f5e71032cf9117b9b193ec030ea0b814d6e289a9

HD Wallet
==================

Mnemonic: gospel oval arm true goat luggage play into artwork sound
marble soft
Base HD Path: m/44'/60'/0'/0/{account_index}

Gas Price
==================
20000000000

Gas Limit
==================
6721975

Listening on 127.0.0.1:8545

Observe from the preceding output:

- Ganache has pre-created 10 user accounts, each with 100 Ethers.

- The section titled "Available Accounts" shows the account addresses of the ten accounts. The section titled "Private Keys" shows the corresponding private keys of each of the ten accounts.

- The Ganache CLI is also listening at a local port with port number 8545.

149

Tip   You will learn how to interact with Ganache through its port in a later section in this chapter.

Graphical User Interface

If you do not want to mess with the command-line interface version of Ganache, you can use the desktop version of it with a graphical user interface. To download the desktop version of Ganache, go to `https://truffleframework.com/ganache` and click the Download button. For the Mac version, you will download a DMG file. Once it is unzipped, simply drag the Ganache icon and drop it onto the Applications folder (see Figure 7-1).

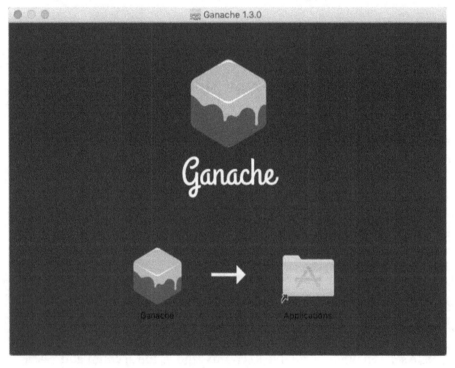

Figure 7-1. *Installing the Ganache on the Mac*

To run it, double-click the Ganache application in the Applications folder. When you start Ganache for the first time, click the Quickstart button. Figure 7-2 shows Ganache up and running. It shows a list of 10 user accounts, each with 100 Ethers.

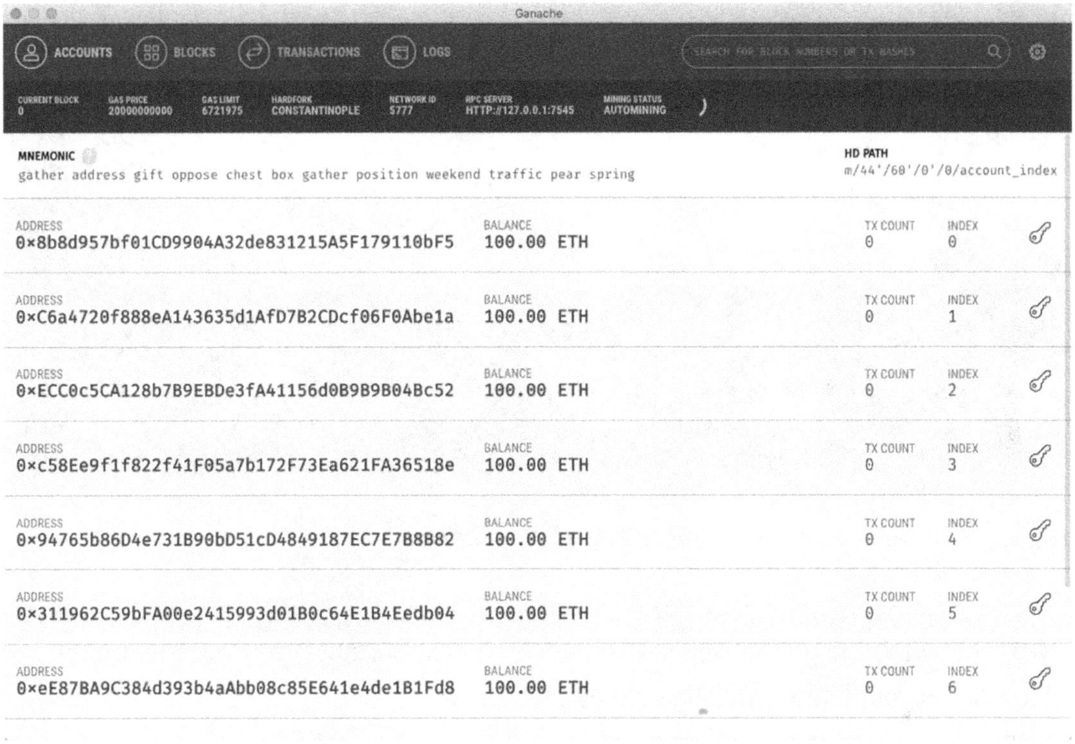

Figure 7-2. *Ganache showing the list of users it has pre-created and the amount of Ethers each account has*

Tip   Observe that for the desktop version of Ganache, it is listening at port 7545 (which you can change), instead of the 8545 in the CLI version of Ganache.

If you want to see the private key of each account, click the key icon displayed next to each account (see Figure 7-3).

Figure 7-3. *Revealing the private key of an account*

Tip   Knowing the private key of each account is important if you want to import that that account into a wallet, such as MetaMask.

When you click the BLOCKS tab, you will see that at the moment there is only one single block (Block 0; see Figure 7-4), which is the genesis block of the blockchain.

Figure 7-4. *Examining the block(s) in the blockchain*

Creating a Smart Contract

Now that you have learned how to install the two different flavors of Ganache, let's now write a Smart Contract and see how you can deploy it onto Ganache. For illustration, I shall use the desktop version of Ganache.

Using the Remix IDE on Chrome, create the following contract and name it as ProofOfExistence.sol:

Caution   For the Remix IDE, ensure that you are loading it using **http** and not **https**. This is because Ganache only accept connections to it using **http**. If you load the Remix IDE using https, you would have problems connecting to Ganache later on.

```solidity
pragma solidity ^0.5.1;

contract ProofOfExistence {

  mapping (bytes32 => bool) private proofs;

  // store a proof of existence in the contract state
  function storeProof(bytes32 proof) private {
    proofs[proof] = true;
  }

  // calculate and store the proof for a document
  function notarize(string memory document) public {
    storeProof(proofFor(document));
  }

  // helper function to get a document's sha256
  function proofFor(string memory document) private
  pure returns (bytes32) {
    return sha256(bytes(document));
  }

  // check if a document has been notarized
  function checkDocument(string memory document) public
  view returns (bool) {
```

```
    return proofs[proofFor(document)];
  }

}
```

The preceding Smart Contract does the following:

- It allows users to pass in a string through the `notarize()` function so that the hash of the string can be stored on the blockchain using the `proofs` state variable (which is of type `mapping`, which is like as associative array).

- It allows users to verify if a string was previously recorded in the blockchain by calling the `checkDocument()` function and checking if the hash of the string exists in the `proofs` state variable.

This Smart Contract acts as a simple notarizer in which a user can store a string (e.g., containing an idea) on the blockchain and proving it later on that this idea was already invented earlier.

Deploying the Contract to Ganache

With the Smart Contract created, you shall now deploy it to Ganache. Under the **Run** tab in the Remix IDE, select **Web3 Provider** as the environment (see Figure 7-5).

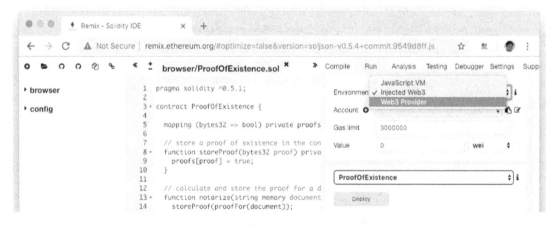

Figure 7-5. *Connecting the Remix IDE to Ganache*

Remix IDE will now prompt you if you want to connect to an Ethereum node. Click OK. In the next screen, enter the Web3 Provider's endpoint URL (see Figure 7-6).

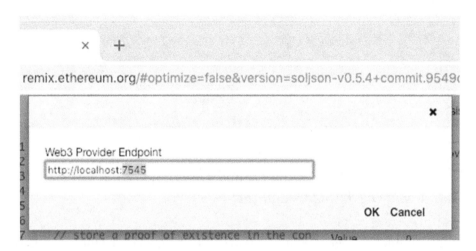

Figure 7-6. *Entering the endpoint URL of Ganache*

The preceding endpoint URL is where the Ethereum node (which is Ganache in this case) is listening at. Recall that desktop version of Ganache is listening at port number 7545. Hence, be sure to specify this port number. If you are using the CLI version of Ganache, the port number is then 8545.

Tip   If you have problems in connecting to the rpc (error message: "Not possible to connect to the Web3 provider. Make sure the provider is running and a connection is open (via IPC or RPC)."), this is likely due to the fact that you are using the **https** version of Remix. To resolve this, simply load Remix using **http**.

Once the Web3 Provider is connected, you can deploy the contract to Ganache. To do so, click the **Deploy** button under the name of the contract (see Figure 7-7).

Tip   Be sure to turn on auto compile in the Remix IDE so that your contract is automatically compiled as you type in the code for the contract.

Figure 7-7. *Deploying the Smart Contract*

Once the contract has been deployed, you should be able to see the two functions (see Figure 7-8).

Figure 7-8. *The Smart Contract deployed with the two functions showing*

Tip   Click the down arrow if you don't see the two functions – notarize and checkDocument.

Examining Ganache

If you now look at Ganache, you will see that the first account has a balance of 99.99 Ethers (see Figure 7-9).

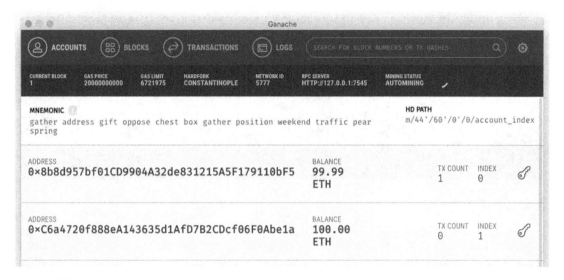

Figure 7-9. *Examining the balance of the first account in Ganache*

This is because when you deploy the contract through Remix IDE, Remix IDE uses the first account (by default) in Ganache to pay for the contract deployment. You can change the account to use in the Remix IDE by selecting the Account to use under the Run tab (see Figure 7-10).

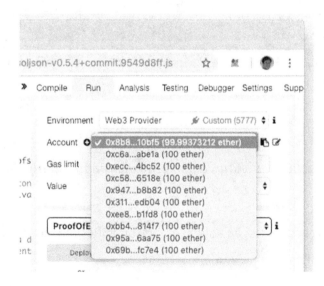

Figure 7-10. *Changing the account to use in the Remix IDE*

Also, under the BLOCKS tab in Ganache, you now see that there is an additional block – Block 1 (see Figure 7-11). This newly created block contains the contract that has been just deployed.

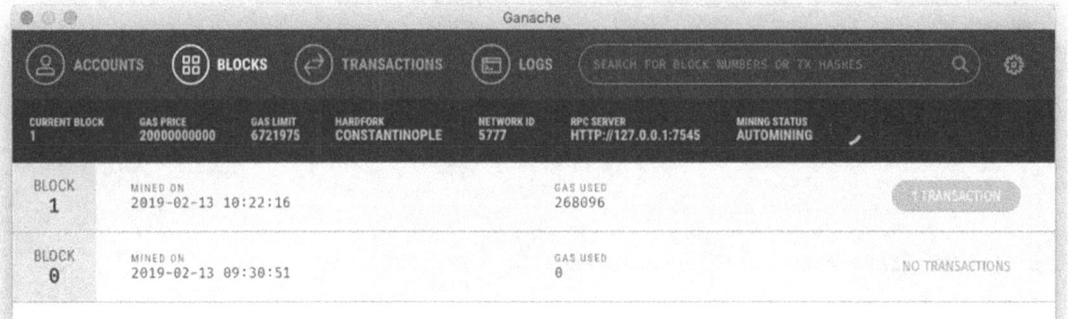

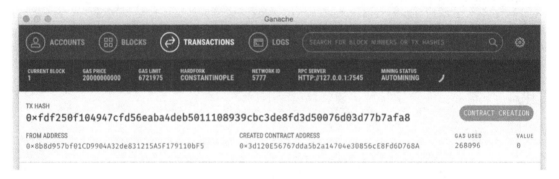

Figure 7-11. *The Ganache blockchain now has an additional block containing the deployed contract*

Under the TRANSACTIONS tab, you would be able to see a new transaction (see Figure 7-12), which is the transaction that deployed the contract.

Figure 7-12. *Ganache now shows a new transaction involving the contract deployment*

In the LOGS tab, you would be able to see the activities that go on behind the scene in Ganache (see Figure 7-13).

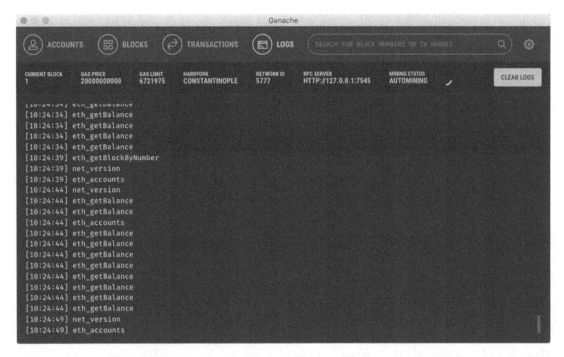

Figure 7-13. *The LOGS tab shows the activities of Ganache behind the scene*

Testing the Contract

Let's now test out the contract. Enter the string "*Hello, Smart Contract!*" into the text box next to the **notarize** button (see Figure 7-14). Then, click the **notarize** button. Next, enter the same string into the text box displayed next to the **checkDocument** button and click the **checkDocument** button. You should be able to see the result "**0: bool:true**". This indicates that the original was stored successfully on the blockchain and then you can verify its existence on the blockchain.

Figure 7-14. *Storing and verifying the existence of the string in the blockchain*

159

If you enter a different string into the text box displayed next to the **checkDocument** button, say "*Hello, Solidity!*" (see Figure 7-15) and then click the **checkDocument** button, you should be able to see the result "**0: bool:false**".

Figure 7-15. *Entering a different string other than the original string will yield a result of false*

If you examine Ganache now, you will be able to see the new block created on the blockchain (see Figure 7-16), as well as the new transaction (which is a contract call) that is performed when you click the notarize button.

Figure 7-16. *Examining Ganache, which has a new block in the blockchain as well as a new transaction*

Connecting MetaMask to Ganache

Since Ganache is a blockchain, you should be able to connect your MetaMask to it. So, let's see how you can do it.

In MetaMask, click the down arrow and select **Custom RPC** (see Figure 7-17).

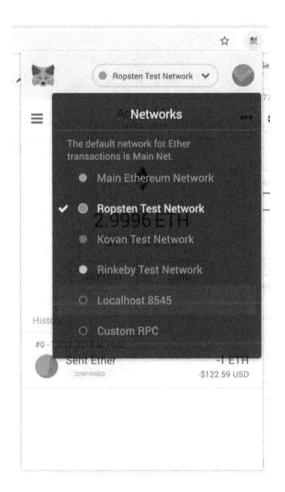

Figure 7-17. *Connecting MetaMask to a custom RPC*

Tip   If you are using the CLI version of Ganache, you can directly select the Localhost 8545 menu item.

You will now see the **Settings** page (see Figure 7-18). Scroll down the page, and under the **New Network** header, enter http://127.0.0.1:7545. This is the endpoint URL that Ganache (desktop version) is listening at. Once this is entered, click the "X" button to close the window.

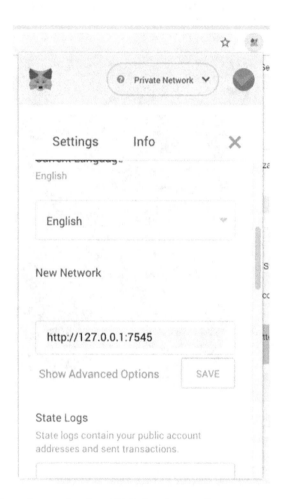

Figure 7-18. *Entering the endpoint URL for Ganache*

When you now click the down arrow again, you will see a new item named
"http://127.0.0.1:7545" (see Figure 7-19). Select it.

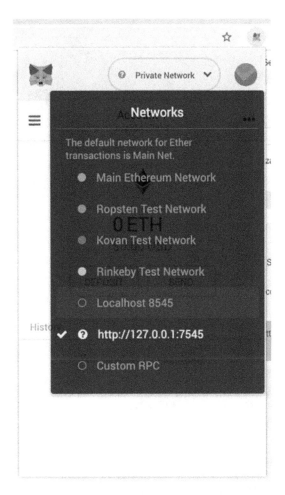

Figure 7-19. *Selecting the newly added RPC to connect to Ganache*

You will now see that your existing account has 0 ETH (see Figure 7-20). This is because your existing account is not valid in this new blockchain (which Ganache is hosting).

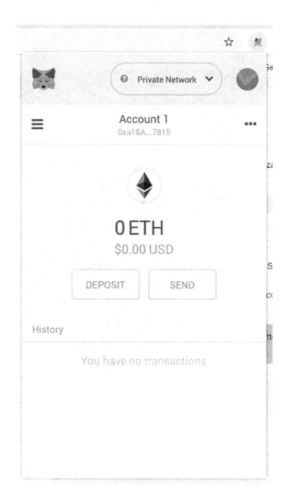

Figure 7-20. *The existing account in MetaMask has no Ethers in the blockchain hosted by Ganache*

You need to import the account(s) from Ganache into MetaMask if you want to see their balance. To do so, click the account icon in MetaMask and select **Import Account** (see Figure 7-21).

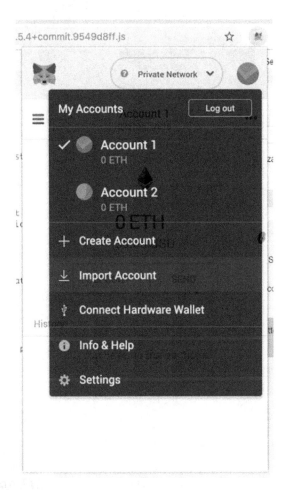

Figure 7-21. *Importing an account in MetaMask*

In the **New Account** page, enter the private key of the first account in Ganache (see Figure 7-22). Then, click **IMPORT**.

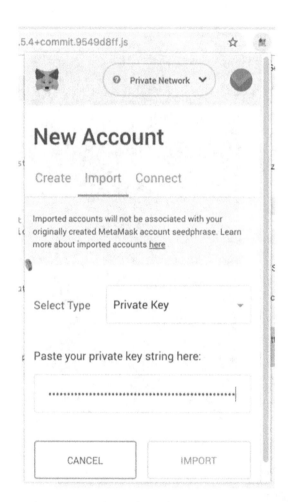

Figure 7-22. *Entering the private key of the first account in Ganache*

The account from Ganache should now be imported into MetaMask (see Figure 7-23).

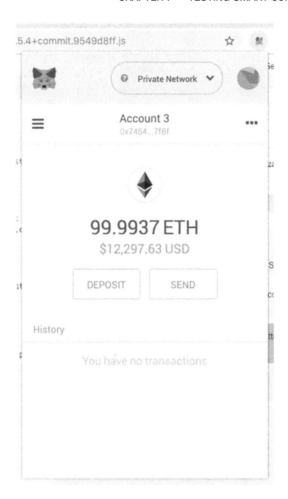

Figure 7-23. *The account in Ganache imported into MetaMask*

You can try to import the other accounts from Ganache into MetaMask. You then send Ethers from one account into another.

The ability to connect MetaMask to Ganache is very useful, especially in later chapters where we talk about interacting with your Smart Contracts via the web3.js APIs.

Summary

In this chapter, you learned how to test your Smart Contract in a stand-alone blockchain hosted by Ganache. Using Ganache allows you to simulate running a blockchain without accessing a real one. And it makes testing your Smart Contracts efficient and effortless.

## CHAPTER 8

Using the web3.js APIs

In the previous chapters, you have learned the basics of Smart Contracts and how to deploy them onto the blockchain. So far, all interactions with the Smart Contracts have been through the Remix IDE. While the Remix IDE provides an easy way for developers to test their Smart Contracts, it is not suitable for use by end users. To allow end users to interact with your Smart Contracts, you need to build front end that hides the complexity of interacting with the Smart Contracts in the back end. For this purpose, you need an API.

In this chapter, you will learn how to interact with Smart Contracts using the web3. js APIs. Using the web3.js APIs, you can build front ends (such as web pages, Node.js applications, etc.) to interact with Smart Contracts.

What Is web3.js?

The web3.js is a collection of libraries that allow you to interact with a local or remote Ethereum node, using HTTP, WebSocket, or IPC. Through the web3.js APIs, your front end can then interact with the Smart Contracts. The web3.js APIs contain the following modules:

- `web3-eth` – For the Ethereum blockchain and smart contracts
- `web3-shh` – For the whisper protocol to communicate p2p and broadcast
- `web3-bzz` – For the swarm protocol, the decentralized file storage
- `web3-utils` – Contains useful helper functions for DApp developers.

For this book, we will only focus on the first module, the `web3-eth`.

© Wei-Meng Lee 2019
W.-M. Lee, *Beginning Ethereum Smart Contracts Programming*,
https://doi.org/10.1007/978-1-4842-5086-0_8

Installing web3.js

Installing **web3.js** requires Node.js. Specifically, you will make use of **npm** to download the web3.js APIs onto your local computer.

Tip   For more information on installing Node.js, check out the following page: `https://nodejs.org/en/download/`.

For this chapter, we shall create a folder named **web3projects** to store the web3.js APIs. In Terminal, type the following commands:

```
$ cd ~
$ mkdir web3projects
$ cd web3projects
```

Before you download the web3.js APIs, you want to create an empty Node.js project:

```
$ npm init --yes
```

The preceding command creates a file named **package.json**. This file contains the dependencies required by a Node.js application. To download the web3.js APIs, type the following command:

```
$ npm install web3@0.20.7 --save
```

Tip   Creating the package.json file will prevent **npm** from showing pages of warning and error messages when you install web3.js.

The `--save` option informs **npm** to modify the **package.json** file and add the **web3.js** as a dependency for the application.

The **web3projects** folder should now have a folder named **node_modules**. Within this **node_modules** folder, you will see a number of folders, all of which make up the suites of APIs that is web3.js.

Testing the web3.js Using MetaMask

With the web3.js downloaded, let's now test it and understand how it works. Create a text file named **TestWeb3.html** and save it in the **web3projects** folder. Populate it as follows:

```
<!DOCTYPE html>
<html lang="en">
<script src="./node_modules/web3/dist/web3.min.js"></script>
<body>
    <script>
        if (typeof web3 !== 'undefined') {
            // this statement is executed if you are using
            // MetaMask
            async function enableAccounts() {
                await ethereum.enable();
                .then((account) => {
                    alert("Account: " + account + "\n" +
                        "Provider Name: " +
                        web3.currentProvider.constructor.name);
                })
            }
            enableAccounts();
        } else {
            // set the provider you want from Web3.providers
            web3 = new Web3(
                new Web3.providers.HttpProvider(
                "http://localhost:8545"));

            alert("Account: " + web3.eth.accounts[0] + "\n" +
                "Provider Name: " +
                web3.currentProvider.constructor.name);
        }
    </script>
</body>
</html>
```

In Terminal, type the following command:

```
$ npm install -g serve
```

Tip   Installing the serve application globally using the -g option may require sudo permission. Alternatively, you can also install it locally within the current directory without using the -g option.

The preceding command installs a web server on the local computer. Typing the serve command in any directory will enable the directory to serve its content through the web server.

In the **web3projects** folder, type the following command:

```
$ serve
```

Using the Chrome browser (with MetaMask installed), load the following URL: http://localhost:5000/TestWeb3.html.

You will see the alert shown in Figure 8-1. Click Connect.

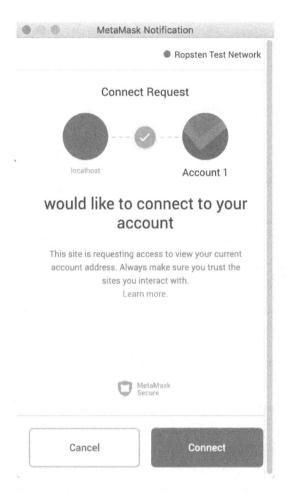

Figure 8-1. *You need to give permission to the page to allow it to access your MetaMask account(s)*

You should now see the alert as shown in Figure 8-2.

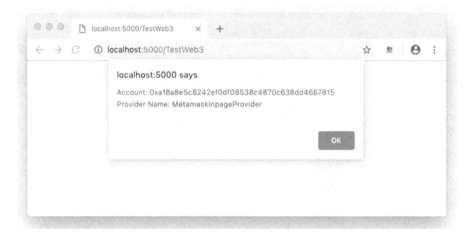

Figure 8-2. *The web3 object connecting to MetaMask*

Let's now understand how this works. First, in your JavaScript code, you first check if web3 is undefined:

```
if (typeof web3 !== 'undefined') {
    // this statement is executed if you are using
    // MetaMask;
    async function enableAccounts() {
        await ethereum.enable()
        .then((account) => {
            alert("Account: " + account + "\n" +
                "Provider Name: " +
                web3.currentProvider.constructor.name);
        })
    }
    enableAccounts();
} else {
```

If you load this page through HTTP on a browser with MetaMask installed, MetaMask will automatically inject the web3 object. This web3 object allows you to interact with an Ethereum node. In this case, it connects to the MetaMask extension on your Chrome browser.

Using the MetaMask extension, you can obtain the address of the accounts. But before the MetaMask extension exposes the accounts, you need to enable it using the `ethereum.enable()` function, like this:

```
async function enableAccounts() {
    await ethereum.enable()
    .then((account) => {
        alert("Account: " + account + "\n" +
            "Provider Name: " +
            web3.currentProvider.constructor.name);
    })
}
enableAccounts();
```

When the user has approved the request to connect to the accounts, you can now get the account address and display it in the alert box.

The `account` object always returns the account you selected in the MetaMask extension in the browser. You can also get the name of the provider using the `web3` object.

Testing the web3.js Without MetaMask

What happens if you load the **TestWeb3.html** page using a non-MetaMask supported browser or if you do not load it using HTTP (i.e., you load the page directly onto the browser)? In this case, the `web3` object will be undefined and the `else` block will now be executed:

```
if (typeof web3 !== 'undefined') {
    ...
} else {
    // set the provider you want from Web3.providers
    web3 = new Web3(
        new Web3.providers.HttpProvider(
        "http://localhost:8545"));

    alert("Account: " + web3.eth.accounts[0] + "\n" +
        "Provider Name: " +
        web3.currentProvider.constructor.name);
}
```

A good solution would be to manually connect to another Ethereum node, such as Ganache. And that's what you will do next.

In Terminal, type the following command to launch Ganache:

```
$ ganache-cli
```

Note   Refer to Chapter 7 if you are not familiar with Ganache.

You should see the following:

```
Ganache CLI v6.4.2 (ganache-core: 2.5.4)

Available Accounts
==================
(0) 0xd5e7d5437cd6279444049ae1b6424737ced0aafe (~100 ETH)
(1) 0xf2bbf643e4a4a6e878eba39f61d353b6a59ad893 (~100 ETH)
(2) 0x26cd848844ca333af7cf8dde0cb1609644eb7b99 (~100 ETH)
(3) 0xdc648ffb58ce6ed2ba4675dfa984f243ac1c0756 (~100 ETH)
(4) 0xe819726440d2c986aef42f9134cd6ee157b31f54 (~100 ETH)
(5) 0x6bef68ce964fe0f7c63894a5bbce58858aba0b33 (~100 ETH)
(6) 0xac6432f160e01731f314bd6506b72446fc95bbc6 (~100 ETH)
(7) 0x55715f224052096b24e3ef2bba71c7f181d35905 (~100 ETH)
(8) 0x1f717912faab85131592439c2c00a7469990bdc9 (~100 ETH)
(9) 0x2adba1a8b9130c112994837fbe3d7595674e8814 (~100 ETH)
...
```

Now, load the **TestWeb3.html** page using either one of the following methods:

- Load the page directly using any web browser.

- Load the page using HTTP on any non-MetaMask supported web browser.

In any of the preceding methods, the web3 object will now connect to Ganache, as shown in Figure 8-3.

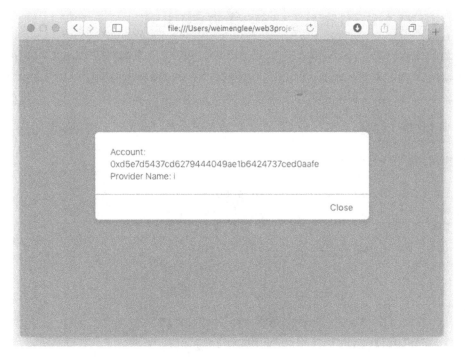

Figure 8-3. *The web3 object connecting to Ganache*

This is because our JavaScript specifically connects to the local Ethereum node listening at port 8545:

```
web3 = new Web3(
    new Web3.providers.HttpProvider(
    "http://localhost:8545"));
```

Tip   For security reasons, MetaMask would only inject the web3 object if the page is loaded using HTTP.

To get the current account address, you could simply specify web3.eth. accounts[0].

Deploying Contracts Using web3.js

The next thing we want to use the web3.js for is to deploy a Smart Contract. For this example, we shall use the same Smart Contract that we have developed in the previous chapter:

```solidity
pragma solidity ^0.5.1;

contract ProofOfExistence {

  mapping (bytes32 => bool) private proofs;

  // store a proof of existence in the contract state
  function storeProof(bytes32 proof) private {
    proofs[proof] = true;
  }

  // calculate and store the proof for a document
  function notarize(string memory document) public {
    storeProof(proofFor(document));
  }

  // helper function to get a document's sha256
  function proofFor(string memory document) private
  pure returns (bytes32) {
    return sha256(bytes(document));
  }

  // check if a document has been notarized
  function checkDocument(string memory document) public
  view returns (bool) {
    return proofs[proofFor(document)];
  }

}
```

Using the Remix IDE, we can get the ABI and the bytecode of the Smart Contract. The ABI is

```
[ { "constant": true, "inputs": [ { "name": "document",
"type": "string" } ], "name": "checkDocument", "outputs": [ { "name": "",
"type": "bool" } ], "payable": false, "stateMutability": "view",
"type": "function" }, { "constant": false, "inputs": [ { "name": "document",
"type": "string" } ], "name": "notarize", "outputs": [], "payable": false,
"stateMutability": "nonpayable", "type": "function" } ]
```

And the bytecode is

```
608060405234801561001057600080fd5b5061033b806100206000396000f3
fe60806040526004361061004657600035 7c010000000000000000000000000
...
8381526020019081526020016000206000061010000a81548160ff0219169083
151502179055505056fea165627a7a72305820273793d02d6109c94bde87c3
d7330575e077c3409d42a3188dcbbadeb54a18260029
```

We want to deploy this Smart Contract onto the Ropsten testnet, through the use of MetaMask. To do so using web3.js, create a new text file named **DeployContract.html** (save it in the **web3projects** folder) and populate it as follows:

```html
<!DOCTYPE html>
<html lang="en">
<script src="./node_modules/web3/dist/web3.min.js"></script>
<body>
    <script>
        let account = "";
        if (typeof web3 !== 'undefined') {
            // this statement is executed if you are using
            // MetaMask;
            async function enableAccounts() {
                await ethereum.enable()
                .then((account) => {
                    account = account;
                })
            }
```

```
            enableAccounts();
        } else {
            // set the provider you want from Web3.providers
            web3 = new Web3(
                new Web3.providers.HttpProvider(
                "http://localhost:8545"));
            account = web3.eth.accounts[0];
        }
        let bytecode =
```
'0x60806040523480156100105760008036fd5b5061033e806100206000396000f3fe60806040
52348015610010576000803fd5b50600436106100365760003560e01c806353fb92331461003
b5780637183616c1461010e575b600080fd5b6100f460048036036020811015610051576000
80fd5b810190808035906020019064010000000081111561006e57600080fd5b82018360208
2011115610080576000803fd5b80359060200191846001830284011164010000000083111715
6100a257600080fd5b91908080601f0160208091040260200160405190810160405280939299
1908181526020018383808284376000818401526001f19601f82011690508083019250505050
505050919291929050505061001c9565b604051808215151515815260200191505060040518
09
10390f35b6101c7600480360360208110156101012457600080fd5b810190808035906020001
90
64010000000081111561014157600080fd5b820183602082011115610153576000803fd5b803
59060200191846001830284011164010000000083111715610175610017557600080fd5b9190
808060
1f016020809104026020016040519081016040528093929190818152602001838380828443760
00081840152601f19601f8201169050808301925050505050505091929192905050506101fa
565b005b60008060006101d78461020e565b815260200190815260200160002060009054906
10100a900460ff169050919050565b61020b6102068261020e565b6102b5565b50565b6000
600282604051808280519060200190808083835b602083106102465780518252602082019150
6
020810190506020830392506102235b600183602003610100a038019825116818451168082
1785525050505050509050019150506020604051808303818559afa158015610288573d600
0803e3d6000fd5b505050604013d602081101561029d57600080fd5b8101908080519060020
0190929190505050509050919050565b600160008083815260200190815260200160002060006
101000a81548160ff0219169083151502179055505056fea265627a7a72305820a8142eeb58
bdc8f3137d990c2e6f31f571e6fff3d8e1ef8881e6a71de963198e64736f6c637828302e352
e31312d6e696768746c792e323031392e362e32352b636f6d6d69742e31636338343735330058';
```
```

```
let abi = [ { "constant": true, "inputs": [ { "name": "document",
"type": "string" } ], "name": "checkDocument", "outputs":
[ { "name": "", "type": "bool" } ], "payable": false,
"stateMutability": "view", "type": "function" }, { "constant":
false, "inputs": [ { "name": "document", "type": "string" } ],
"name": "notarize", "outputs": [], "payable": false,
"stateMutability": "nonpayable", "type": "function" } ];
let contract = web3.eth.contract(abi);
web3.eth.estimateGas({data: bytecode},
    function(error, result){
        if (!error){
            contract.new(
                {
                    from : account,
                    data : bytecode,
                    gas : result
                }, function (err, contract) {
                    if (err) {
                        alert(err);
                        return;
                    } else if (contract.address){
                        alert('Contract address: '
                            + contract.address);
                    }
                });
        } else {
            alert('err = ' + error);
        }
    }
);

</script>
</body>
</html>
```

As you can observe from the preceding code, we did the following:

- Connect to the Ethereum node.

- Get the primary account associated with the node.

- Declare a variable containing the bytecode of the contract and another variable containing the ABI of the contract.

- Use the **web3.eth.contract()** function to create a contract using the ABI of the contract.

- Use the **web3.eth.estimateGas()** function to estimate the gas required to deploy the contract onto the blockchain.

- Once the gas estimate is obtained, use the new() function to deploy the contract. You need to pass in the following – the account to use for deploying the contract, the bytecode of the contract, and the gas estimate (maximum amount of gas allowed).

- Once the contract is deployed, you can now print out the address of the contract

Let's test the page to see if it works. Using Chrome, load the page using this URL: http://localhost:5000/DeployContract.html. Once the page is loaded, you should see MetaMask prompting you to confirm the transaction (see Figure 8-4). Note the estimated gas needed to deploy the contract is 0.000272 ETH. Click CONFIRM.

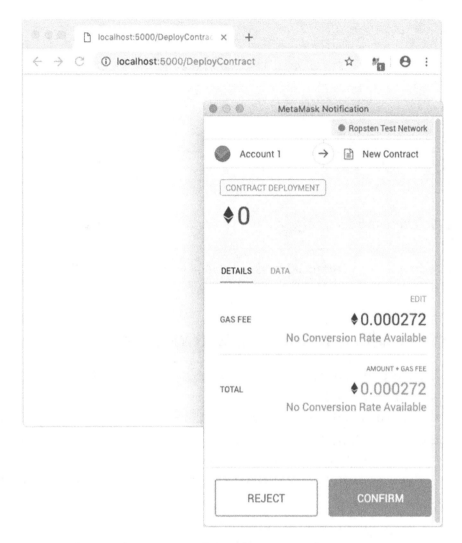

Figure 8-4. *Deploying the contract through MetaMask*

After a while, once the block containing the transaction is mined, you will see the alert showing you the address of the contract (see Figure 8-5).

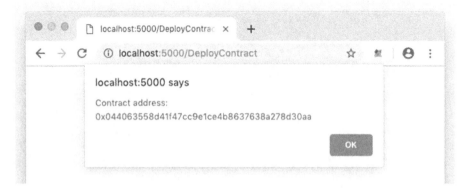

Figure 8-5. *Our contract has been deployed and with its address shown*

In this example, the contract address is 0x044063558d41F47cC9e1CE4B8637638a278 D30aA.

Interacting with a Contract Using web3.js

In the previous section, you saw how you used web3.js to deploy a Smart Contract onto the Ethereum blockchain. Besides using it to deploy contract, web3.js is often used to build front ends so that users can interact with your Smart Contract directly. And hence in this section, you will learn how to use web3.js to interact with your newly deployed contract. For our illustration, we shall build a web front end.

Create a new text file and name it as **main.css**. Populate the file with the following:

```
body {
    background-color:#F0F0F0;
    padding: 2em;
    font-family: 'Raleway','Source Sans Pro', 'Arial';
}
.container {
    width: 95%;
    margin: 0 auto;
}
label {
    display:block;
    margin-bottom:10px;
```

184

```
        font-weight: bold;
}
input {
        padding:10px;
        width: 100%;
        margin-bottom: 1em;
}
button {
        margin: 2em 0;
        padding: 1em 4em;
        display:block;
        font-size: medium;
}
#result {
        padding:1em;
        background-color:#fff;
        margin: 1em 0;
}
```

This file will serve as the CSS for the web front end that you will build next. Create a new text file and name it as **DocumentNotarizer.html** (save it in the **web3projects** folder). Populate it with the following:

```
<!DOCTYPE html>
<html lang="en">
<head>
        <title>Document Notarizer</title>
        <link rel="stylesheet" type="text/css" href="main.css">
        <script src="./node_modules/web3/dist/web3.min.js">
        </script>
</head>
<body>
        <div class="container">
                <h1>Document Notarizer</h1>
                <label class="col-lg-2 control-label">
                Document to notarize</label>
```

```
    <input id="document1" type="text">
    <button id="btnNotarize">Notarize</button>
    <label class="col-lg-2 control-label">
    Check Document</label>
    <input id="document2" type="text">
    <button id="btnCheck">Check</button>
    <label class="col-lg-2 control-label">Status</label>
    <h2 id="result"></h2>
</div>
<script src=
    "https://code.jquery.com/jquery-3.2.1.slim.min.js">
</script>
<script>
    if (typeof web3 !== 'undefined') {
        // this statement is executed if you are using
        // MetaMask
        async function enableAccounts() {
            await ethereum.enable()
        }
        enableAccounts();
    } else {
        // set the provider you want from Web3.providers
        web3 = new Web3(
            new Web3.providers.HttpProvider(
            "http://localhost:8545"));
    }

    let abi = [ { "constant": true, "inputs": [ { "name": "document",
    "type": "string" } ], "name": "checkDocument", "outputs": [ {
    "name": "", "type": "bool" } ], "payable": false, "stateMutability":
    "view", "type": "function" }, { "constant": false, "inputs": [ {
    "name": "document", "type": "string" } ], "name": "notarize",
    "outputs": [], "payable": false, "stateMutability": "nonpayable",
    "type": "function" } ];
```

```
    var contract = web3.eth.contract(abi);
    var notarizer = contract.at(
        '0x044063558d41F47cC9e1CE4B8637638a278D30aA');

    $("#btnNotarize").click(function() {
        notarizer.notarize($("#document1").val(),
        (error, result) => {
            $("#result").html(result);
        });
    });

    $("#btnCheck").click(function() {
        notarizer.checkDocument($("#document2").val(),
        (error, result) => {
            if(!error) {
                $("#result").html(result.toString());
            } else
                console.error(error);
        });
    });
    </script>
</body>
</html>
```

In Terminal, ensure that the serve command is still running (if not, type serve in the **web3projects** folder). Load the Chrome web browser with the following URL: http://localhost:5000/DocumentNotarizer.html. You should see the page as shown in Figure 8-6.

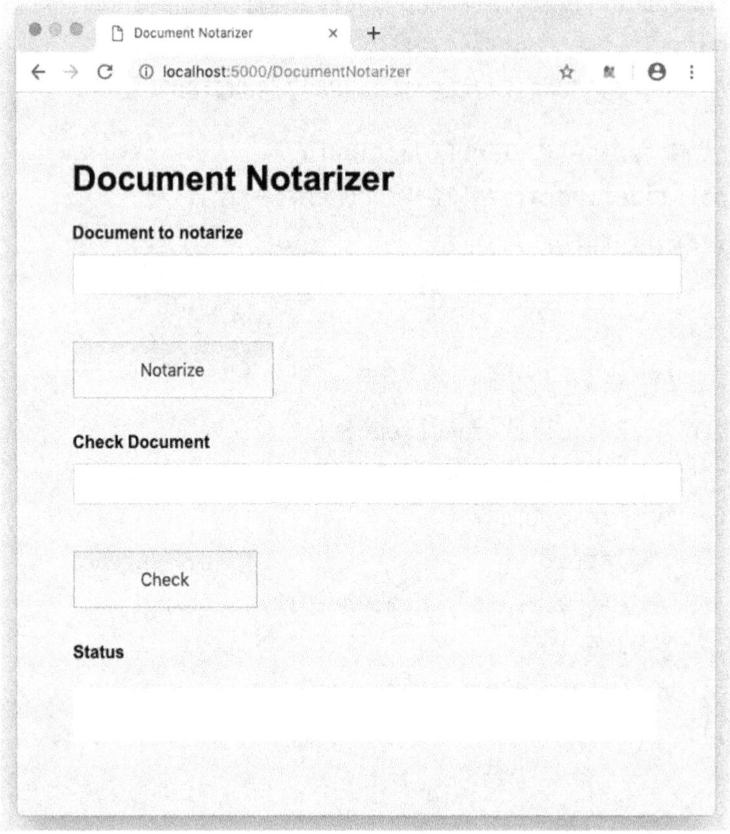

Figure 8-6. *The web front end to interact with the Smart Contract*

Enter a string in the first text box and then click the **Notarize** button. You should see the pop-up by MetaMask (see Figure 8-7).

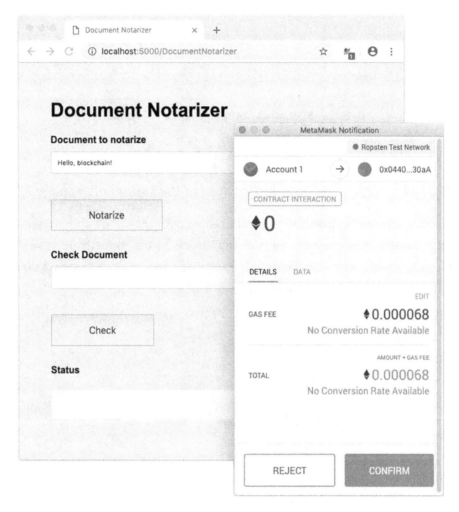

Figure 8-7. *Confirming the transaction to send the string to the Smart Contract for notarization*

Click **CONFIRM** to confirm the transaction. When the transaction is sent, you will immediately see the transaction hash displayed at the bottom of the page (see Figure 8-8).

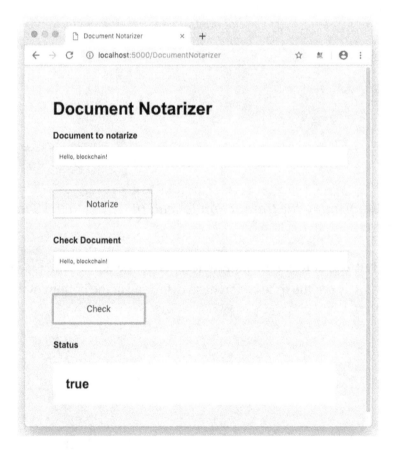

Figure 8-8. *The transaction hash is displayed at the bottom of the page*

Once the block containing the transaction is mined, you will be able to type the same string in the second text box and then click the **Check** button to verify if the same string was previously stored on the blockchain. If the string was saved previously, you should see **true** in the bottom of the screen (see Figure 8-9).

Figure 8-9. *Verifying if a string was previous stored on the blockchain*

Let's see how the code works. First, when the **Notarize** button is clicked, you call the notarize() function of the contract (which is called notarizer) and pass it the value of the text box:

```
notarizer.notarize($("#document1").val(),
(error, result) => {
    $("#result").html(result);
});
```

Notice that you pass in a callback function to the notarize() function so that when the transaction is confirmed by the user, you can get the transaction hash, which is then displayed in the label at the bottom of the page.

Likewise, to verify a string, you call the checkDocument() function with the string to verify, together with the callback function:

```
notarizer.checkDocument($("#document2").val(),
(error, result) => {
    if(!error) {
        $("#result").html(result.toString());
    } else
        console.error(error);
});
```

When the result is returned back to you, you will display it in the label.

Sending Ethers to Smart Contracts

Our ProofOfExistence contract provides a free service to let people notarize their documents on the blockchain (users just need to pay for gas required to write data onto the blockchain).

In a real commercial setting, you might want to charge for this service. For example, anytime a user wants to write to the blockchain, you want to charge a service fee. In the following example, you will modify the contract so that calls to the notarize() function require a payment of 1 Ether.

For simplicity, you shall deploy the contract from the Remix IDE onto the Ropsten testnet directly (instead of using the web3.js). Here is the modified contract (in bold):

```solidity
pragma solidity ^0.5.1;

contract ProofOfExistence {

  mapping (bytes32 => bool) private proofs;

  // store a proof of existence in the contract state
  function storeProof(bytes32 proof) private {
    proofs[proof] = true;
  }

  // calculate and store the proof for a document
  function notarize(string memory document) public payable {
    require(msg.value == 1 ether);
    storeProof(proofFor(document));
  }

  // helper function to get a document's sha256
  function proofFor(string memory document) private
  pure returns (bytes32) {
    return sha256(bytes(document));
  }

  // check if a document has been notarized
  function checkDocument(string memory document) public
  view returns (bool) {
    return proofs[proofFor(document)];
  }
}
```

The require() function in Solidity allows you to check for certain condition. In this particular example, it checks that the call to the notarize() function is accompanied with exactly 1 Ether. If not, the transaction will fail and all unused gas will be refunded back to the caller. Note that you must add the payable keyword to the end of the function declaration.

Let's now deploy the contract using the Remix IDE (see Figure 8-10).

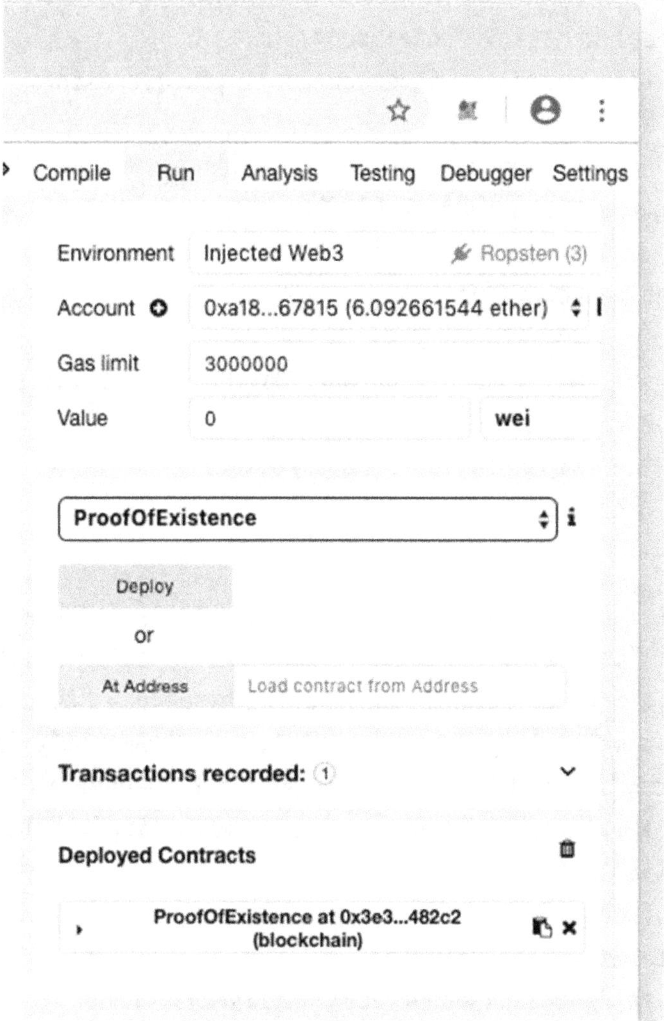

Figure 8-10. *Deploying the modified Smart Contract using the Remix IDE*

When the contract is deployed, copy the address of the new contract. The address for the modified contract is now 0x3e3d5b0282c49d8e9e211b8fdc9225ec43d482c2.

Since the contract has been modified, you would also need to modify the **DocumentNotarizer.html** file. Add in the following statements in bold to the **DocumentNotarizer.html** file:

...

```
    if (typeof web3 !== 'undefined') {
        // this statement is executed if you are using
        // MetaMask
        async function enableAccounts() {
            await ethereum.enable()
        }
        enableAccounts();
    } else {
        // set the provider you want from Web3.providers
        web3 = new Web3(
            new Web3.providers.HttpProvider(
            "http://localhost:8545"));
    }

    let abi = [ { "constant": false, "inputs": [ { "name": "document",
    "type": "string" } ], "name": "notarize", "outputs": [],
    "payable": true, "stateMutability": "payable", "type": "function" },
    { "constant": true, "inputs": [ { "name": "document", "type": "string"
    } ], "name": "checkDocument", "outputs": [ { "name": "", "type":
    "bool" } ], "payable": false, "stateMutability": "view", "type":
    "function" } ];
    var contract = web3.eth.contract(abi);
    var notarizer = contract.at(
        '0x3e3d5b0282c49d8e9e211b8fdc9225ec43d482c2');

    $("#btnNotarize").click(function() {
        notarizer.notarize($("#document1").val(),
        {
          gas: 300000,
          from: web3.eth.accounts[0],
          value: 1000000000000000000
        },
        (error, result) => {
            $("#result").html(result);
        });
    });
```

```
$("#btnCheck").click(function() {
    notarizer.checkDocument($("#document2").val(),
    (error, result) => {
        if(!error) {
            $("#result").html(result.toString());
        } else
            console.error(error);
    });
});
```
...

There are three things that you need to modify:

- The ABI of the new contract. The notarize() function now has a new signature, so the ABI must be updated.

- The address of the newly deployed contract.

- A JSON string containing the amount of Ether to be sent to the contract. Here, we specified that the maximum amount of gas required is 300000 (all unused gas will be refunded), and it is to be deducted from the account in the Ethereum node (such as MetaMask or Ganache). Finally, the amount of Ether to be sent to the contract is specified in Wei (1000000000000000000 Wei is equivalent to 1 Ether).

Once the HTML file is updated, load the Chrome browser with this URL: http://localhost:5000/DocumentNotarizer.html. As usual, enter a string to notarize and click the **Notarize** button. You will now see the pop-up from MetaMask (see Figure 8-11).

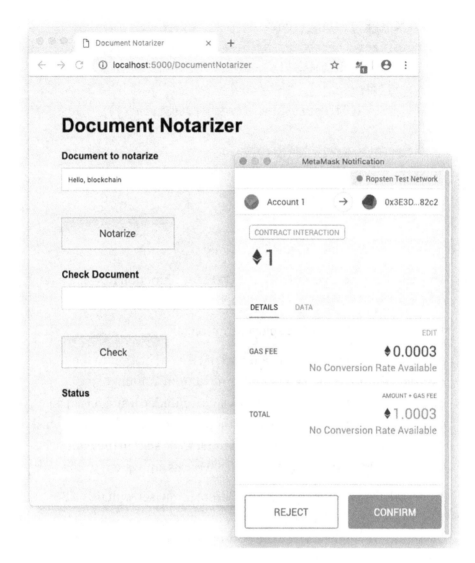

Figure 8-11. *Sending a payment of 1 Ether to the contract when you notarize a string*

Observe that you will be sending 1 Ether to the contract, and the gas fee is 0.0003 Ether (based on the estimated 300,000 gas and gas price of 1 Gwei per unit). Click CONFIRM.

Tip   1 Ether = 1,000,000,000 Gwei, so 300,000 gas would cost 300,000,000,000,000 Gwei, which is equal to 0.0003 Ether. You can vary the price of gas in MetaMask by clicking the Edit button in Figure 8-11 and then clicking the Advanced tab (see Figure 8-12).

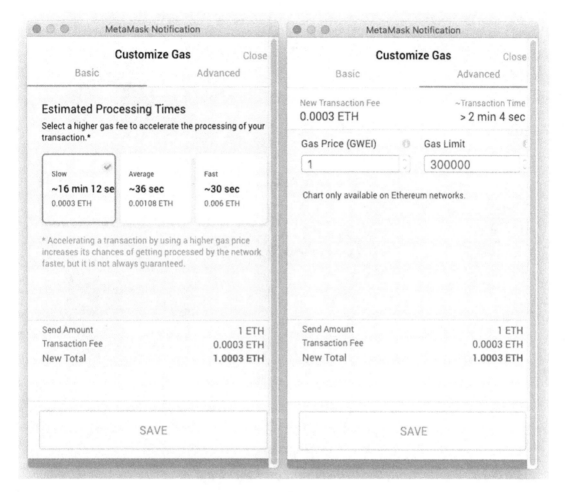

Figure 8-12.   *Varying the price of gas in MetaMask*

Once the transaction is confirmed and mined, you can check Etherscan to verify that 1 Ether has indeed been transferred to the contract (see Figure 8-13).

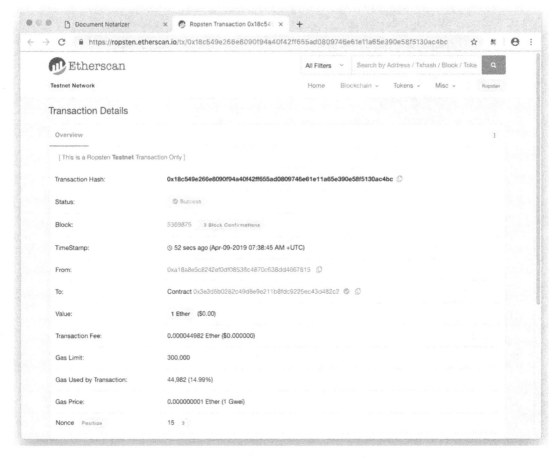

Figure 8-13. *Confirming the transaction on Etherscan*

Summary

In this chapter, you learned how to use the web3.js APIs to interact with your Smart Contracts. You learned how to deploy Smart Contracts programmatically using web3.js. In addition, you also used the web3.js to build a web front end, and you saw how you can send Ethers to a Smart Contract.

CHAPTER 9

Smart Contract Events

In the previous chapter, you saw how to use web3.js to interact with your deployed Smart Contract. Using web3.js, you were able to connect to an Ethereum node (through MetaMask, or directly to an Ethereum node such as Ganache running locally on your computer). Using the document notarizer example, you were able to

- Send a string to the Smart Contract through the web front end for storing its hash on the blockchain

- Send Ethers to the Smart Contract to pay for the notarization service

- Verify if a string's hash has been previously stored on the blockchain

However, there are a number of important features that have been missing:

- We need to inform the user if the string they are trying to notarize has already been saved in the blockchain.

- We need to inform the user after the string has been successfully saved in the blockchain.

- We also need to inform the user if the amount of Ether they sent to the contract is not of the correct amount.

So in this case, it is clear that there must be a communication mechanism to feed back to the user of the Smart Contract when certain events occur. And this is the focus of this chapter.

What Are Events in Solidity?

In Solidity, your Smart Contract can emit events so that whoever is interested in handling them can listen for it. To define an event, you give a name to the event and prefix it with the event keyword, like this:

© Wei-Meng Lee 2019
W.-M. Lee, *Beginning Ethereum Smart Contracts Programming*,
https://doi.org/10.1007/978-1-4842-5086-0_9

```
//---an event in Solidity---
event DocumentNotarized(
  address from,
  string text,
  bytes32 hash
);
```

Tip   You are free to define the parameters of your event.

In the preceding example, DocumentNotarized is an event in Solidity. The parameters in the event – from, text, and hash – allow the Smart Contract to pass data back to the event listener.

To fire an event, use the emit keyword, followed by the event name, and the arguments to pass to the event, for example:

```
emit DocumentNotarized(msg.sender, document,
    proofFor(document));
```

Adding Events to the ProofOfExistence Contract

Using the ProofOfExistence contract that we have been using for the previous two chapters, let's now add some events to the contract and see how we can make use of events to make our Smart Contract smarter:

```
pragma solidity ^0.5.1;

contract ProofOfExistence {

  mapping (bytes32 => bool) private proofs;

  //---events---
  event DocumentNotarized(
    address from,
    string text,
    bytes32 hash
  );
```

```
event NotarizationError(
  address from,
  string text,
  string reason
);
```

```
// store a proof of existence in the contract state
function storeProof(bytes32 proof) private {
  proofs[proof] = true;
}
```

```
// calculate and store the proof for a document
function notarize(string memory document) public payable {

  //---check if string was previously stored---
  if (proofs[proofFor(document)]) {
      //---fire the event---
      emit NotarizationError(msg.sender, document,
          "String was stored previously");

      //---refund back to the sender---
      msg.sender.transfer(msg.value);

      //---exit the function---
      return;
  }

  if (msg.value != 1 ether) {
      //---fire the event---
      emit NotarizationError(msg.sender, document,
          "Incorrect amount of Ether paid");

      //---refund back to the sender---
      msg.sender.transfer(msg.value);

      //---exit the function---
      return;
  }

  //---store the hash of the string---
  storeProof(proofFor(document));
```

```
    //---fire the event---
    emit DocumentNotarized(msg.sender, document,
        proofFor(document));
}

// helper function to get a document's sha256
function proofFor(string memory document) private
pure returns (bytes32) {
    return sha256(bytes(document));
}

// check if a document has been notarized
function checkDocument(string memory document) public
view returns (bool) {
    return proofs[proofFor(document)];
}
}
```

In the preceding modifications, we did the following:

- Added two events – DocumentNotarized and NotarizationError.

- Before a document (string) can be notarized, it is first checked to see if the hash of the document already exists on the blockchain. If it does, the document cannot be notarized. In this case, you will fire the NotarizationError event to inform the user of this error. In this case, you also need to refund the user the Ether that was sent along this transaction, since the notarization was not successful. You do so using the msg.sender.transfer() function. The msg.value property contains the amount of Ether sent by the user.

- The next check you need to perform is to ensure that the user sends exactly 1 Ether. If the user does not send the exact amount, the transaction is also rejected and you will fire the NotarizationError event to inform the user of the reason. Likewise, you will need to refund the user of the amount sent.

- The DocumentNotarized event will be fired when a document has been successfully notarized.

Observe that in both events – `NotarizationError` and `DocumentNotarized`, we have the `from` parameter. This is because when an event is fired, it is sent to all event handlers listening for the event. The `from` parameter provides a way for event handlers to know if events raised are relevant to them. You will see its use in the next section.

Deploying the Contract

With the modified Smart Contract, deploy it using the Remix IDE. Once it is deployed, take note of its address (see Figure 9-1).

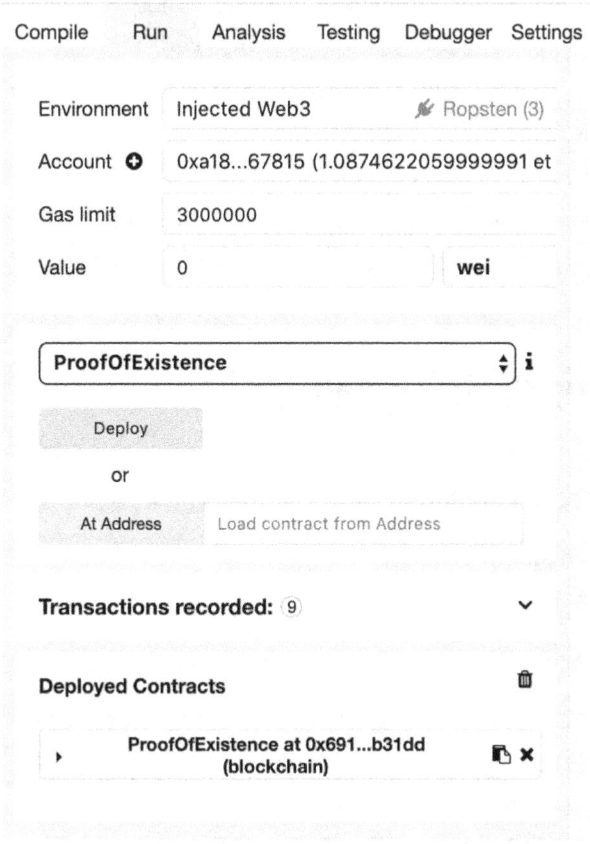

Figure 9-1. *Deploying the modified contract in Remix IDE*

For this example, the new contract address is 0x6910022c777ff4c35aabb5e2aba65 f2ffe4b31dd. Also, since we have added events to the Smart Contract, we need to get the new ABI of the contract so that you can use it in your front end in the next section. The new ABI for this contract is

```
[ { "constant": true, "inputs": [ { "name": "document", "type": "string" } ],
"name": "checkDocument", "outputs": [ { "name": "", "type": "bool" } ],
"payable": false, "stateMutability": "view", "type": "function" },
{ "constant": false, "inputs": [ { "name": "document", "type": "string" } ],
"name": "notarize", "outputs": [], "payable": true, "stateMutability": "payable",
"type": "function" }, { "anonymous": false, "inputs": [ { "indexed": false,
"name": "from", "type": "address" }, { "indexed": false, "name": "text",
"type": "string" }, { "indexed": false, "name": "hash", "type": "bytes32" } ],
"name": "DocumentNotarized", "type": "event" }, { "anonymous": false,
"inputs": [ { "indexed": false, "name": "from", "type": "address" },
{ "indexed": false, "name": "text", "type": "string" }, { "indexed": false,
"name": "reason", "type": "string" } ], "name": "NotarizationError",
"type": "event" } ]
```

Handling Events Using web3.js

With the events defined in the Smart Contract, we can now learn how to handle events in our front end using web3.js. To handle an event, first create an instance of the event, like this:

```
var documentNotarizedEvent =
    notarizer.DocumentNotarized();
```

Then, use the watch() function with a callback to listen for events:

```
documentNotarizedEvent.watch(function(error, result) {
    if (!error){
        if (result.args.from ==
            web3.eth.defaultAccount){
            $("#result").html("Document: " +
                result.args.text +
                " notarized as: " + result.args.hash);
        }
    }
});
```

The `result` argument in the callback function will contain a property named `args`, which in turn contains the parameters defined in your event. In the `DocumentNotarized` event, it will contain a reference to `from`, `text`, and `hash`. As mentioned earlier, when an event is fired, all clients listening to the events will be invoked. Hence it is important that you handle events only relevant to yourself. In this case, we checked the `from` argument and update the UI only if the value of the `from` argument is the same as the current account address.

Let's now modify the **DocumentNotarizer.html** file with the following statements in bold and save it as **DocumentNotarizerEvents.html** (save it in the **web3projects** folder):

```
<!DOCTYPE html>
<html lang="en">
<head>
    <title>Document Notarizer</title>
    <link rel="stylesheet" type="text/css" href="main.css">
    <script src="./node_modules/web3/dist/web3.min.js">
    </script>
</head>
<body>
    <div class="container">
        <h1>Document Notarizer</h1>
        <label class="col-lg-2 control-label">
        Document to notarize</label>
        <input id="document1" type="text">
        <button id="btnNotarize">Notarize</button>
        <label class="col-lg-2 control-label">
        Check Document</label>
        <input id="document2" type="text">
        <button id="btnCheck">Check</button>
        <label class="col-lg-2 control-label">Status</label>
        <h2 id="result"></h2>
    </div>
    <script src="https://code.jquery.com/jquery-3.2.1.slim.min.js"></script>
```

```
<script>
    if (typeof web3 !== 'undefined') {
        // this statement is executed if you are using
        // MetaMask
        async function enableAccounts() {
            await ethereum.enable();
        }
        enableAccounts();
    } else {
        // set the provider you want from Web3.providers
        web3 = new Web3(
            new Web3.providers.HttpProvider(
                "http://localhost:8545"));
    }

    let abi = [ { "constant": true, "inputs": [ { "name": "document",
    "type": "string" } ], "name": "checkDocument", "outputs": [ { "name":
    "", "type": "bool" } ], "payable": false, "stateMutability": "view",
    "type": "function" }, { "constant": false, "inputs": [ { "name":
    "document", "type": "string" } ], "name": "notarize", "outputs": [],
    "payable": true, "stateMutability": "payable", "type": "function" },
    { "anonymous": false, "inputs": [ { "indexed": false, "name": "from",
    "type": "address" }, { "indexed": false, "name": "text", "type":
    "string" }, { "indexed": false, "name": "hash", "type": "bytes32"
    } ], "name": "DocumentNotarized", "type": "event" }, { "anonymous":
    false, "inputs": [ { "indexed": false, "name": "from", "type":
    "address" }, { "indexed": false, "name": "text", "type": "string" },
    { "indexed": false, "name": "reason", "type": "string" } ], "name":
    "NotarizationError", "type": "event" } ];
    var contract = web3.eth.contract(abi);
    var notarizer = contract.at(
        '0x6910022c777ff4c35aabb5e2aba65f2ffe4b31dd');

    var documentNotarizedEvent =
        notarizer.DocumentNotarized();
```

```
documentNotarizedEvent.watch(function(error, result) {
    if (!error){
        if (result.args.from ==
            web3.eth.defaultAccount){
            $("#result").html("Document: " +
                result.args.text +
                " notarized as: " + result.args.hash);
        }
    }
});

var notarizationErrorEvent =
    notarizer.NotarizationError();

notarizationErrorEvent.watch(function(error, result) {
    if (!error){
        if (result.args.from ==
            web3.eth.defaultAccount){
            $("#result").html(
                "Error. <br/> Document: " +
                result.args.text +
                "<br/> Reason: " + result.args.reason);
        }
    }
});

$("#btnNotarize").click(function() {
    notarizer.notarize($("#document1").val(),
    {
      gas: 300000,
      from: web3.eth.accounts[0],
      value: 100000000000000000
    },
```

```
        (error, result) => {
            $("#result").html(
                "Notarization pending confirmation...");
        });
    });

    $("#btnCheck").click(function() {
        notarizer.checkDocument($("#document2").val(),
        (error, result) => {
            if(!error) {
                $("#result").html(result.toString());
            } else
                console.error(error);
        });
    });
    </script>
</body>
</html>
```

Testing the Front End

To test the front end, load Chrome with the following URL: http://localhost:5000/
DocumentNotarizerEvents.html.

Caution   Ensure that the serve command is running in the **web3projects** folder.

Enter a string to notarize and click the **Notarize** button. You will see the pop-up from
MetaMask (see Figure 9-2).

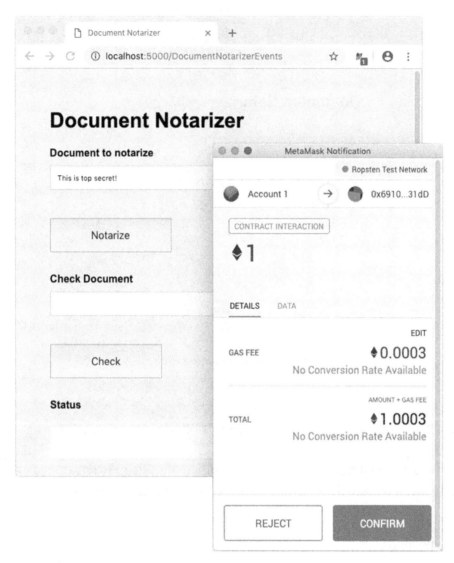

Figure 9-2. *Notarizing a string*

Click **CONFIRM** to confirm the transaction. You will immediately see the message displayed in the label on the bottom of the page (see Figure 9-3).

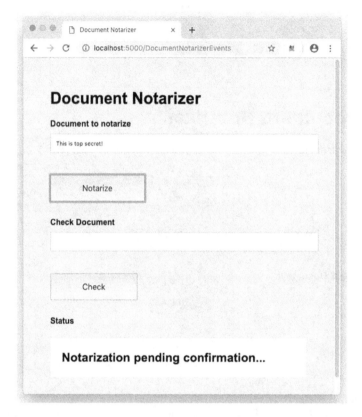

Figure 9-3. *The transaction (notarization) is pending confirmation*

When block containing the transaction is mined, the `DocumentNotarized` event will be fired, and you will see the message displayed as shown in Figure 9-4.

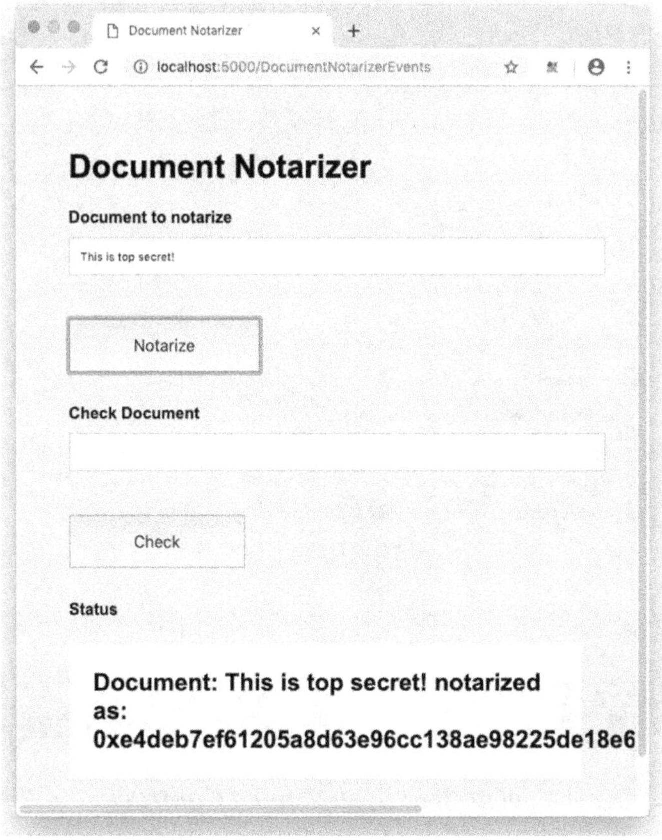

Figure 9-4. *The document is notarized and its hash is returned via the event*

In the `https://ropsten.etherscan.io` page, locate the page for the contract (which in this example is 0x6910022c777ff4c35aabb5e2aba65f2ffe4b31dd), and click the latest transaction hash (TxHash). Click the **Event Logs** tab and you should be able to see the event that was fired (see Figure 9-5).

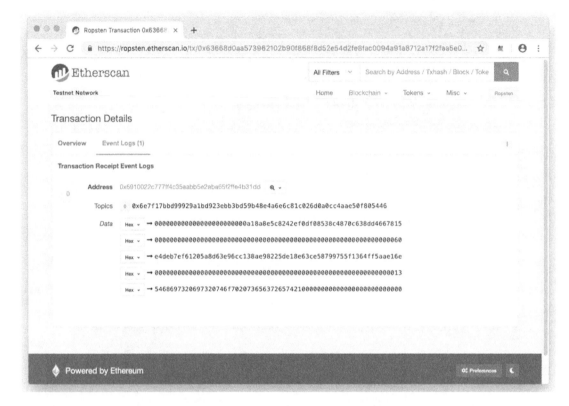

Figure 9-5. *Locating the event fired by the Smart Contract*

The **Data** section contains the data that is logged together with the event. By default all the data is displayed in hexadecimal (Hex) format, but you can change to display as number, text, or address. Figure 9-6 shows the relevant parts of the Data section displayed in the different formats.

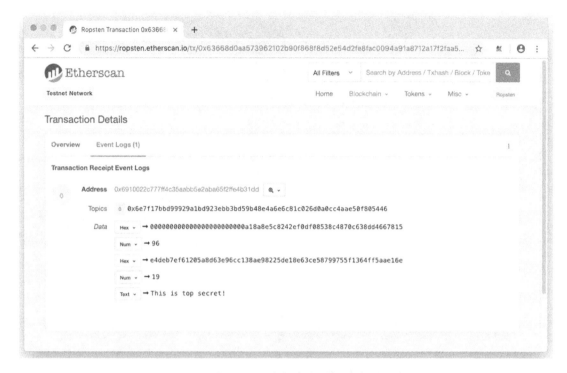

Figure 9-6. *Viewing the data for the event displayed in the different format*

Tip   You don't really need to understand the data logged in the Data section. The web3.js will encapsulate all the arguments in the event.

Notarizing the Same Document Twice

If you click the **Notarize** button one more time to notarize the same string again, you will now get the error as shown in Figure 9-7 (after the block containing the transaction has been mined).

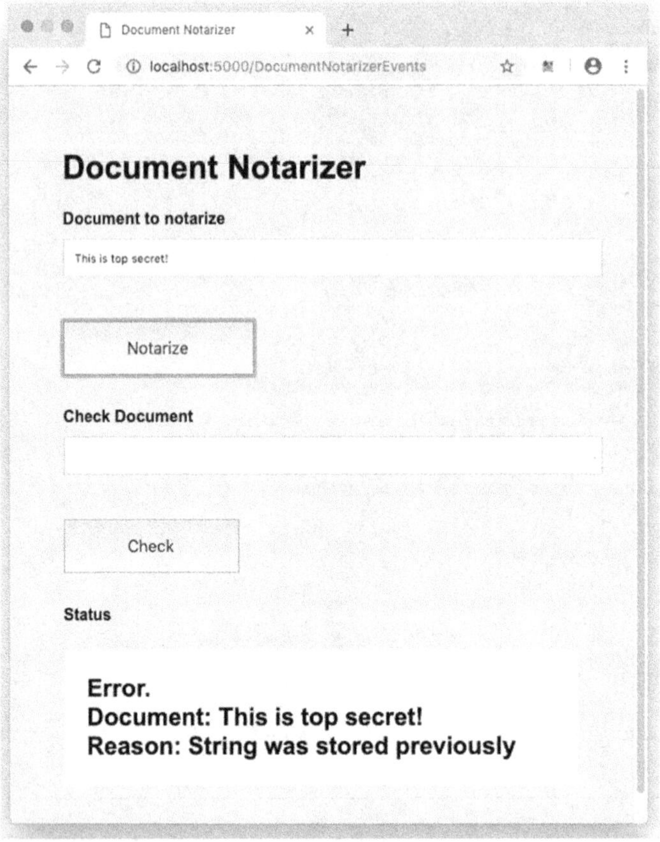

Figure 9-7. *The notarization failed because it was previously notarized*

This is because the hash of the string already exists on the blockchain, and hence the NotarizationError event was fired:

```
//---check if string was previously stored---
if (proofs[proofFor(document)]) {
    //---fire the event---
    emit NotarizationError(msg.sender, document,
        "String was stored previously");

    //---refund back to the sender---
    msg.sender.transfer(msg.value);

    //---exit the function---
    return;
}
```

Observe that besides firing the `NotarizationError` event, the contract also calls the `msg.sender.transfer()` function to refund the amount (`msg.value`) back to the user (`msg.sender`). In the next section, you will see the proof that the amount was indeed refunded back to the user.

Sending Incorrect Amount of Ether

The last scenario that we want to try out is when the wrong amount of Ether is sent to the contract. To do so, we modify the **DocumentNotarizerEvents.html** file and send 0.9 Ether (instead of 1 Ether) to the contract:

```
$("#btnNotarize").click(function() {
    notarizer.notarize($("#document1").val(),
    {
      gas: 300000,
      from: web3.eth.accounts[0],
      value: 900000000000000000
    },
    (error, result) => {
        $("#result").html(
            "Notarization pending confirmation...");
    });
});
```

To test this, load the Chrome browser with the following URL: `http://localhost:5000/DocumentNotarizerEvents.html`, and enter a string to notarize. Click the **Notarize** button, and you should see MetaMask displaying a pop-up (see Figure 9-8).

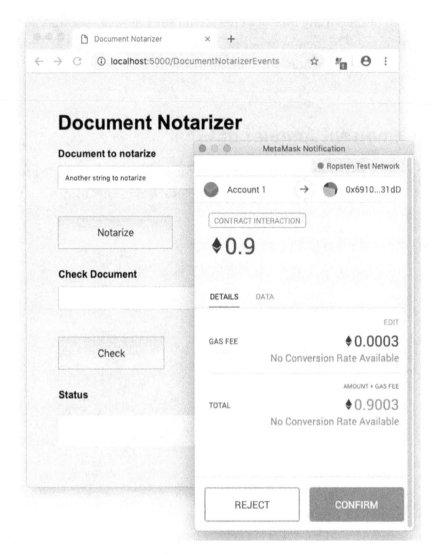

Figure 9-8. *Sending insufficient amount of Ether to a Smart Contract*

Observe that you will be sending 0.9 Ether over to the contract. Click **CONFIRM**.
When the block containing the transaction is mined, you should see the error message
as shown in Figure 9-9.

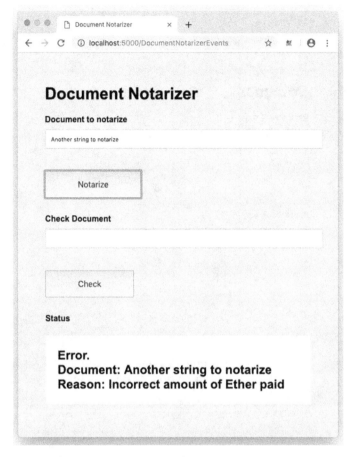

Figure 9-9. *The event fired to reflect the insufficient amount of Ether sent*

What happened to the 0.9 Ether that was sent to the contract? To find out, go to MetaMask and click the arrow icon showing the latest transaction (see Figure 9-10).

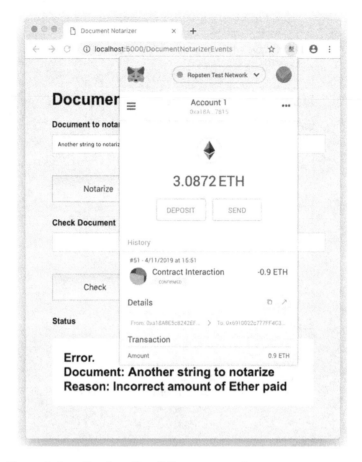

Figure 9-10. *Examining the details of the transaction*

This will bring up the Etherscan page. In particular, focus on the section labeled **To:** (see Figure 9-11).

Figure 9-11. *The internal transfer made within the Smart Contract for the refund*

Observe that there is an internal transfer of 0.9 Ether from the contract back to the account which sent the Ether. This is the refund that is performed by the contract:

```
if (msg.value != 1 ether) {
    //---fire the event---
    emit NotarizationError(msg.sender, document,
        "Incorrect amount of Ether paid");

    //---refund back to the sender---
    msg.sender.transfer(msg.value);

    //---exit the function---
    return;
}
```

Summary

In this chapter, you learned how Smart Contracts can fire events so that front-end applications that are interacting with them can handle them. Using events, you have made your document notarizer Smart Contract must more usable. In the next chapter, we will put all that we have learned about Smart Contract to build a lottery application.

CHAPTER 10

Project – Online Lottery

Now that you have seen how Smart Contract works and how to interact with them through the use of the web3.js APIs, it is now a good time to explore an application from end to end – from the Smart Contract to the front end, and perhaps give you some ideas for building your own decentralized applications.

How the Lottery Game Works

For this chapter, we will build a lottery game using a Smart Contract. For this contract, we will allow players to place a bet on a number. Figure 10-1 shows how the game works.

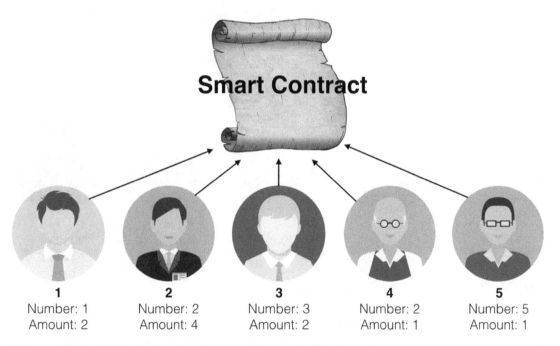

1	2	3	4	5
Number: 1	Number: 2	Number: 3	Number: 2	Number: 5
Amount: 2	Amount: 4	Amount: 2	Amount: 1	Amount: 1

Figure 10-1. *How the online lottery game works*

© Wei-Meng Lee 2019
W.-M. Lee, *Beginning Ethereum Smart Contracts Programming*,
https://doi.org/10.1007/978-1-4842-5086-0_10

In the figure, there are a total of five players. Each player will place a bet on a number. For example, player 1 bets on the number 1 using 2 Ethers, and player 2 bets on the number 2 with 4 Ethers, and so on. The contract will randomly draw a number when the maximum number of players is reached. In this example, the contract will draw the winning number after the fifth players have betted.

Suppose the winning number is 2. Based on the example, players 2 and 4 have betted on the winning number. The amount won by each winner will be proportionate to how much they have betted. The calculation is shown in Figure 10-2.

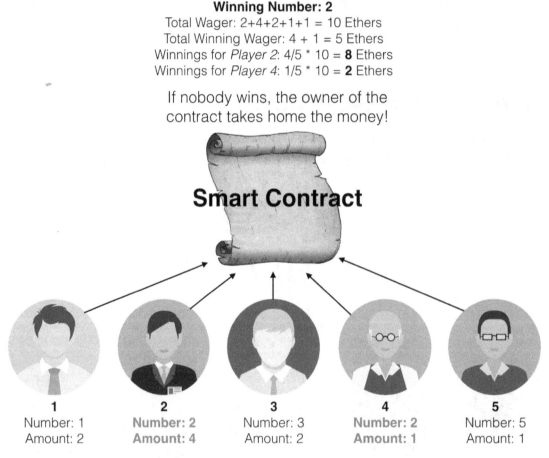

Figure 10-2. *Calculating the winnings of each player*

Our contract will automatically transfer the payout to the winners. If there is no winner for the game, all the Ethers will be transferred to the owner of the contract.

Defining the Smart Contract

For the next few sections, we shall walk through the creation of the contract so that you can see how it is built. For building this contract, we shall use the Remix IDE.

First, define the contract called Betting:

```
pragma solidity ^0.5;

contract Betting {

}
```

Let's declare some variables:

```
contract Betting {
    address payable owner;
    uint minWager = 1;
    uint totalWager = 0;
    uint numberOfWagers = 0;
    uint constant MAX_NUMBER_OF_WAGERS = 2;
    uint winningNumber = 999;
    uint constant MAX_WINNING_NUMBER = 3;
    address payable [] playerAddresses;
    mapping (address => bool) playerAddressesMapping;
    struct Player {
        uint amountWagered;
        uint numberWagered;
    }
    mapping(address => Player) playerDetails;
}
```

Here is the use of each variable:

- owner is used to store the address of the account that deployed the contract.

- minWager stores the minimum amount of Ether that a player needs to wager.

- totalWager stores the total amount of Ethers all the players have wagered so far in a game.

- `totalNumberOfWagers` stores the total number of players who have played in the game so far.

- `MAX_NUMBER_OF_WAGERS` lets you define the maximum number of players allowed in a game before the winning number is drawn. For ease of testing, we have set it to 2. In real life, this could be set to a much larger number.

- `winningNumber` stores the winning number for the lottery. When it is set to 999, it indicates that the winning number has not been drawn yet.

- `MAX_WINNING_NUMBER` defines the maximum winning number for the lottery game. The winning number is from 1 to `MAX_WINNING_NUMBER`.

- `playerAddresses` is an array storing the account address of each player. You prefix the declaration with the `payable` keyword to indicate that each player is able to send/receive Ether.

- Besides storing the player account address in the array, you also store them in a mapping object – `playerAddressesMapping`. This is mainly for performance reason. When you need to search for a particular player address, it is much more efficient to search through a `mapping` object rather than iterate through all the elements in an array. This is especially true if you have a large number of players in a game.

- `Player` is a structure that contains two members – `amountWagered` and `numberWagered`

- `playerDetails` is another mapping object that stores the details of each player's waging details.

Constructor

For the lottery game, you need to set the minimum amount needed for each bet. To make the contract versatile, you can allow this value to be set when the contract is deployed. To do so, you can pass in the value through the contract's constructor.

The constructor for the `Betting` contract takes in an integer value, indicating the minimum amount of Ether needed to bet on a number:

```
// the constructor for the contract
constructor(uint _minWager) public {
    owner = msg.sender;
    if (_minWager >0) minWager = _minWager;
}
```

In the constructor, we also saved the address of the account that deployed the account.

Note   For simplicity, we are specifying the minimum wager amount to be in Ether.

Betting a Number

Next, let's define the bet() function. The bet() function allows a player to bet on a number:

```
function bet(uint number) public payable {
    // you check using the mapping for performance reasons
    require(playerAddressesMapping[msg.sender] == false);

    // check the range of numbers allowed
    require(number >=1 && number <= MAX_WINNING_NUMBER);

    // note that msg.value is in wei; need to convert to
    // ether
    require( (msg.value / (1 ether)) >= minWager);

    // record the number and amount wagered by the player
    playerDetails[msg.sender].amountWagered = msg.value;
    playerDetails[msg.sender].numberWagered = number;

    // add the player address to the array of addresses as
    // well as mapping
    playerAddresses.push(msg.sender);
    playerAddressesMapping[msg.sender] = true;

    numberOfWagers++;
    totalWager += msg.value;
```

```
        if (numberOfWagers >= MAX_NUMBER_OF_WAGERS) {
            announceWinners();
        }
    }
```

Note   Observe that the bet() function has the payable keyword. This means that when a player bets on a number, he must also send in Ethers.

In this function, you need to perform a number of checks. First, ensure that each player can only bet once by checking that the player address does not already exist in the playerAddressesMapping object:

```
require(playerAddressesMapping[msg.sender] == false);
```

Next, you need to check that the number betted falls within the range allowed:

```
require(number >=1 && number <= MAX_WINNING_NUMBER);
```

You also need to check that the amount betted is at least the minimum amount. Since msg.value contains the amount in Wei, you need to convert it to Ether:

```
require( (msg.value / (1 ether)) >= minWager);
```

Once all these checks are cleared, you need to record the number and amount wagered by the player (msg.sender is the address of the player):

```
playerDetails[msg.sender].amountWagered = msg.value;
playerDetails[msg.sender].numberWagered = number;
```

You would also add the player address to the array of addresses as well as the mapping object:

```
playerAddresses.push(msg.sender);
playerAddressesMapping[msg.sender] = true;
```

You also need to increment the number of wagers as well as sum up all the amount wagered so far:

```
numberOfWagers++;
totalWager += msg.value;
```

Finally, you check if the required number of players have been met. If it has, you will announce the winner (which you will define in the next section):

```
if (numberOfWagers >= MAX_NUMBER_OF_WAGERS) {
    announceWinners();
}
```

Drawing the Winning Number and Announcing the Winners

The next function to define is announceWinners(). The announceWinners() function draws a random number and calculates the winning for each player and transfers the winnings to them:

```
function announceWinners() private {
    winningNumber =
      uint(keccak256(abi.encodePacked(block.timestamp))) %
      MAX_WINNING_NUMBER + 1;

    address payable[MAX_NUMBER_OF_WAGERS] memory winners;

    uint winnerCount = 0;
    uint totalWinningWager = 0;

    // find out the winners
    for (uint i=0; i < playerAddresses.length; i++) {
        // get the address of each player
        address payable playerAddress =
            playerAddresses[i];

        // if the player betted number is the winning
        // number
        if (playerDetails[playerAddress].numberWagered ==
            winningNumber) {
            // save the player address into the winners
            // array
            winners[winnerCount] = playerAddress;
```

```
                // sum up the total wagered amount for the
                // winning numbers
                totalWinningWager +=
                  playerDetails[playerAddress].amountWagered;
                winnerCount++;
            }
        }

        // make payments to each winning player
        for (uint j=0; j<winnerCount; j++) {
            winners[j].transfer(
                (playerDetails[winners[j]].amountWagered /
                 totalWinningWager) * totalWager);
        }
    }
}
```

Because Solidity code runs on multiple nodes and must be deterministic, it is not possible to generate truly random numbers. We need a way to generate a random number that can be used by all other nodes running the same code. To solve this, one way is to use the `block.timestamp` constant, which it is assigned by miner:

```
winningNumber =
  uint(keccak256(abi.encodePacked(block.timestamp))) %
  MAX_WINNING_NUMBER + 1;
```

The preceding statement will generate a random number between 1 and `MAX_WINNING_NUMBER`. Once it is generated and assigned to `winningNumber`, it will be the same for all other nodes which run the same contract.

Tip An alternative to determining the winning number using block number is to access an external web service. In real life, you may want to connect to a real lottery feed.

You next create an array in memory to store all the winning players:

```
address payable[MAX_NUMBER_OF_WAGERS] memory winners ;
```

You will iterate through all the players using the playerAddresses array and check if the number they wagered on is the winning number. The winning players are then added to the winners array:

```
for (uint i=0; i < playerAddresses.length; i++) {
    address payable playerAddress =
        playerAddresses[i];
    if (playerDetails[playerAddress].numberWagered ==
        winningNumber) {
        winners[winnerCount] = playerAddress;
        totalWinningWager +=
            playerDetails[playerAddress].amountWagered;
        winnerCount++;
    }
}
```

Finally, calculate the winnings for each player and transfer the winnings to them using the transfer() function:

```
// make payments to each winning player
for (uint j=0; j<winnerCount; j++) {
    winners[j].transfer(
        (playerDetails[winners[j]].amountWagered /
        totalWinningWager) * totalWager);
}
```

Getting the Winning Number

To allow the outside world to know the winning number, add the following function named getWinningNumber():

```
function getWinningNumber() view public returns (uint) {
    return winningNumber;
}
```

Killing the Contract

When there are no winners for the game, the Smart Contract will hold the Ethers that were sent to it. In order to send the Ethers back to the account that deploys the contract, you need to kill (destruct) the contract. This is done via the kill() function:

```
function kill() public {
    if (msg.sender == owner) {
        selfdestruct(owner);
    }
}
```

Obviously, you need to ensure that only the owner (the one that deploys the contract) of the contract can kill it. When the contract is killed, all Ethers can automatically be transferred back to the owner.

Testing the Contract

With the contract created, it is now time to deploy it and test it using the Remix IDE. For deployment, we shall use Account 1 in MetaMask.

In the Remix IDE, type 1 next to the **Deploy** button and then click the **Deploy** button (see Figure 10-3). The 1 indicates that the minimum amount you need to bet for a number is 1 Ether.

Figure 10-3. *Setting the constructor for the contract*

Click **CONFIRM** to deploy the contract (see Figure 10-4).

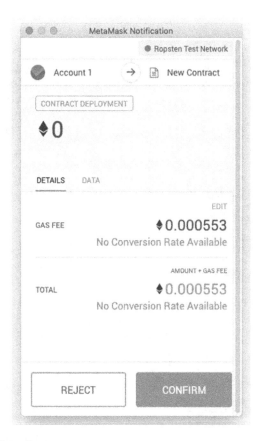

Figure 10-4. *Deploying the contract*

Betting on a Number

Once the transaction is confirmed, enter 2 next to the **bet** button and enter 2 next to the **Value** label and select the unit as **ether** (see Figure 10-5). This means that you are now betting on the number 2 using 2 Ethers.

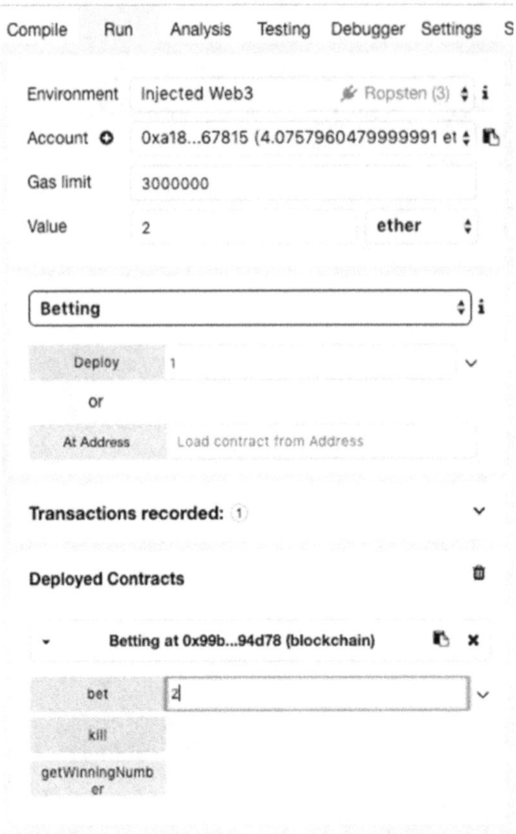

Figure 10-5. *Using Account 1 to bet on a number with the amount of Ether specified*

Tip   Remember to set the **Value** and the unit to **ether**

Click the **bet** button to place the bet. MetaMask will display a pop-up asking you to confirm the transaction. Note the 2 Ethers you are sending to the contract (see Figure 10-6). Click **CONFIRM**.

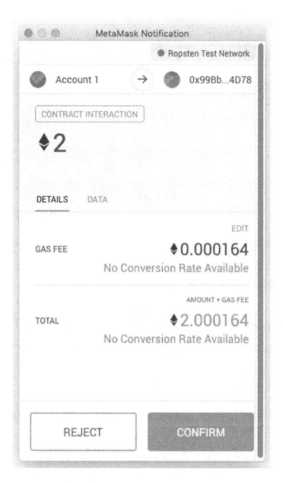

Figure 10-6. *Observe the amount of Ethers you are sending*

At this moment, you can record the current balance of Account 1 (see Figure 10-7). For my example, my Account 1 now has a balance of 2.0756 Ethers.

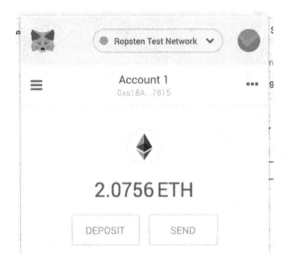

Figure 10-7. *Take note of the balance of Account 1*

In MetaMask, switch to Account 2 now. Back in the Remix IDE, now bet on the number 1 using 3 Ethers (see Figure 10-8). Click the **bet** button and confirm the transaction.

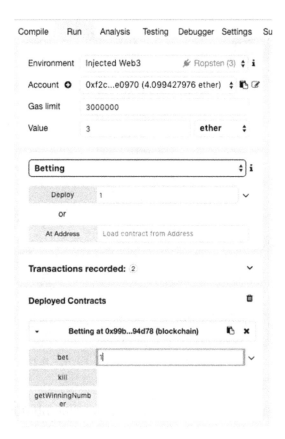

Figure 10-8. *Using Account 2 to bet on another number with the amount of Ethers specified*

Record the current balance of Account 2. For my example, balance for Account 2 stands at 1.0993 Ethers (see Figure 10-9).

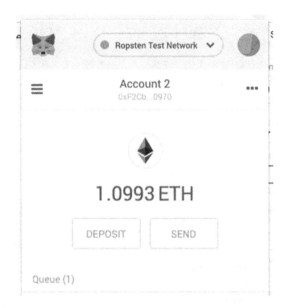

Figure 10-9. *Take note of the balance of Account 2*

After the transaction has been confirmed, the winning number would be drawn.

Note   Remember that our contract will draw a winning number after the second player has placed a bet.

Viewing the Winning Number

Click the **getWinningNumber** button to check the winning number (see Figure 10-10). In my example here, the winning number is 2, which means that Account 1 has won the lottery. Since there is only one winner, Account 1 will take all the Ethers betted, which is 5 (2+3) Ethers.

Figure 10-10. *Checking on the winning number*

When you now go back to Account 1 in MetaMask, you will see that the balance is now updated with the additional Ethers (see Figure 10-11).

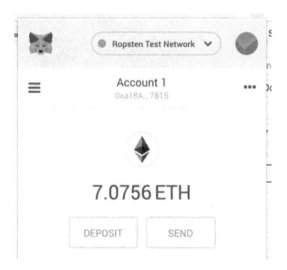

Figure 10-11. *Account 1 balance is now updated with the winnings*

Examining the Contract on Etherscan

If you examine the details of the Smart Contract in Etherscan, you will be able to see that the contract now has a balance of 0 Ether (see Figure 10-12).

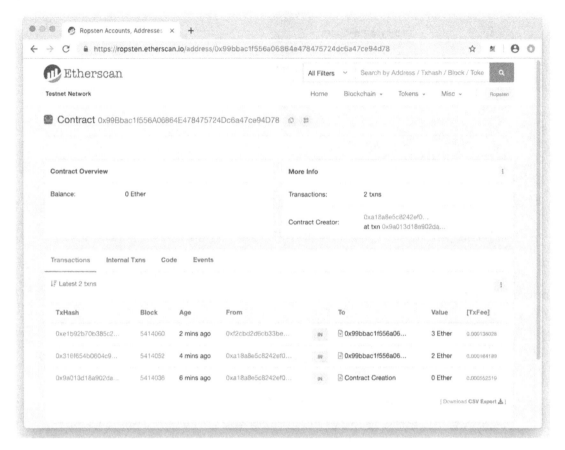

Figure 10-12. *Examining the balance of the contract on Etherscan*

If you click the **Internal Txns** tab, you will see that there is an internal transfer of 2 Ethers to Account 1 (see Figure 10-13).

Parent TxHash	Block	Age	From	To	Value
0xe1b92b70b385c2...	5414060	2 mins ago	0x99bbac1f556a06...	0xa18a8e5c8242ef0...	5 Ether

[Download **CSV Export** ⬇]

Figure 10-13. *The contract recorded an internal transfer of Ethers to the winner of the game*

Killing the Contract

In the previous section, you saw that in my example one player won the game and the contract transferred all the winnings to the player. If you try the previous section yourself, you may encounter one of the following scenarios:

- One player wins the game, just like what was illustrated in the previous section.

- Both players win the game (both betted on the same winning number). In this case the contract will transfer the winnings to the players based on the number of Ethers they have betted.

- No player wins the game. In this case the Ethers betted by both players would be held by the contract.

In this section, we shall examine the last scenario where no one wins the game and how to get back the Ethers held by the contract.

To ensure that no one wins the game, let's hard code the winning number in the contract:

```
function announceWinners() private {
    /*
    winningNumber =
      uint(keccak256(abi.encodePacked(block.timestamp))) %
      MAX_WINNING_NUMBER + 1;
    */
    winningNumber = 1;
```

So now the winning number is always 1, and as long as no player bets on 1, there will be no winners.

As in the previous section, in the Remix IDE, deploy the contract using Account 1. After the contract is deployed, observe the balance of Account 1 (see Figure 10-14).

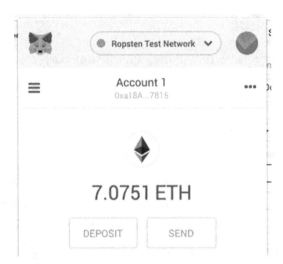

Figure 10-14. *Take note of the balance of Account 1*

Using Account 2, bet the number 2 with 1 Ether. After that, using Account 3, bet the number 3 with 1 Ether. After the winning number has been drawn (which is always 1), check the details of the contract on Etherscan (see Figure 10-15).

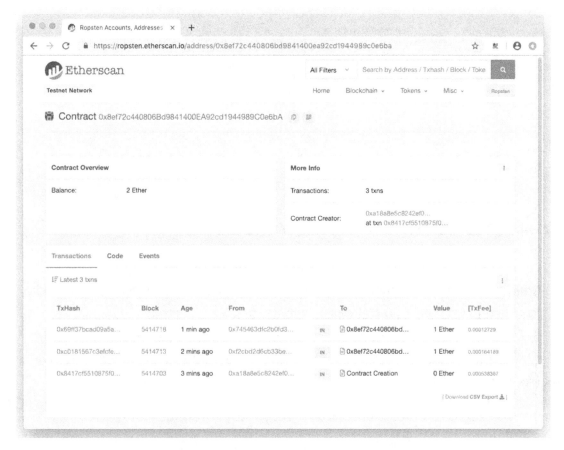

Figure 10-15. *Examining the balance of the contract on Etherscan*

Observe that the contract has a balance of 2 Ethers (since no player wins). So how do you get the 2 Ethers back? Turns out that if you kill the contract, the Ethers would be refunded back to the account that deploys it.

So let's now switch back to Account 1 in the MetaMask. In the Remix IDE, click the **kill** button (see Figure 10-16).

Figure 10-16. *Killing the contract in the Remix IDE*

Caution   Only the account that deployed the contract can kill it. Hence you need to switch to Account 1 (in MetaMask) in order to kill the contract.

Once the transaction is confirmed, you should see the 2 Ethers credited into Account 1 (see Figure 10-17).

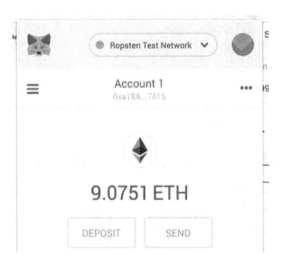

Figure 10-17. *The Ethers would be credited back into Account 1 after the contract has been killed*

In the Etherscan entry for the contract, you will an internal transfer from the contract to the original account that deployed the contract (see Figure 10-18).

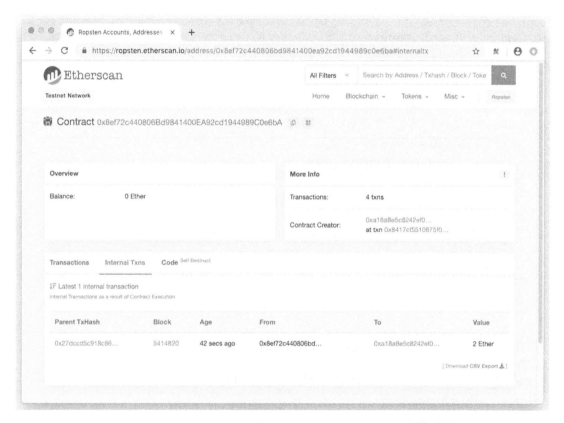

Figure 10-18. *Verifying that the balance Ether was transferred back to the owner of the contract*

Adding Events to the Contract

Up to till point, our contract has all its functions defined. But to be truly usable, you need to define a couple of events so that you can notify the users when certain events happen:

- When the winning number is announced

- When there is a change in the game status (e.g., the number of players played so far)

Add the following statements in bold to the Betting contract in the Remix IDE:

```solidity
pragma solidity ^0.5;

contract Betting {
    address payable owner;
    uint minWager = 1;
    uint totalWager = 0;
    uint numberOfWagers = 0;
    uint constant MAX_NUMBER_OF_WAGERS = 2;
    uint winningNumber = 999;
    uint constant MAX_WINNING_NUMBER = 3;

    address payable [] playerAddresses;

    mapping (address => bool) playerAddressesMapping;
    struct Player {
        uint amountWagered;
        uint numberWagered;
    }

    mapping(address => Player) playerDetails;

    // the event to announce the winning number
    event WinningNumber(
        uint number
    );

    // the event to display the status of the game
    event Status (
        uint players,
        uint maxPlayers
    );

    // the constructor for the contract
    constructor(uint _minWager) public {
        owner = msg.sender;

        // set the minimum amount wager amount allowed
        // note that this number is in ether
```

```
    if (_minWager >0) minWager = _minWager;
}

function bet(uint number) public payable {
    // ensure that each player can play once
    // you check using the mapping for performance reasons
    require(playerAddressesMapping[msg.sender] == false);

    // check the range of numbers allowed
    require(number >=1 && number <= MAX_WINNING_NUMBER);

    // note that msg.value is in wei; need to convert to
    // ether
    require( (msg.value / (1 ether)) >= minWager);

    // record the number and amount wagered by the player
    playerDetails[msg.sender].amountWagered = msg.value;
    playerDetails[msg.sender].numberWagered = number;

    // add the player address to the array of addresses as
    // well as mapping
    playerAddresses.push(msg.sender);
    playerAddressesMapping[msg.sender] = true;

    numberOfWagers++;
    totalWager += msg.value;

    if (numberOfWagers >= MAX_NUMBER_OF_WAGERS) {
        announceWinners();
    }
    // call the event to inform the client about the
    // status of the game
    emit Status(numberOfWagers, MAX_NUMBER_OF_WAGERS);
}

function announceWinners() private {
    //winningNumber =
    //uint(keccak256(abi.encodePacked(block.timestamp))) %
    //    MAX_WINNING_NUMBER + 1;
```

245

```
        // hard code the winning number to see what happens
        // when the contract is killed
        winningNumber = 1;

        // call the event to announce the winning number
        emit WinningNumber(winningNumber);

        address payable[MAX_NUMBER_OF_WAGERS] memory winners ;

        uint winnerCount = 0;
        uint totalWinningWager = 0;

        // find out the winners
        ...
    }
    function getWinningNumber() view public returns (uint) {
        return winningNumber;
    }
    function kill() public {
        if (msg.sender == owner) {
            selfdestruct(owner);
        }
    }
    function getStatus() view public returns (uint,uint) {
        return (numberOfWagers, MAX_NUMBER_OF_WAGERS);
    }
}
```

Note that you added two events and fire them when

- Someone has betted a number

- Announcing the winning number

Also observe that we added a function named getStatus() so that when a client connects to the Smart Contract for the first time, it can query the contract to find out the current status of the game.

You can now redeploy the contract (with the constructor value 1). Once the contract is deployed, take note of its address and ABI. You will need it in the next section.

Creating the Web Front End

Let's now create the web front end for the lottery game. Create a new text file and name it as **OnlineBetting.html.** Save it in the **web3projects** folder.

Populate the **OnlineBetting.html** file as follows:

```
<!DOCTYPE html>
<html lang="en">
<head>
    <meta charset="UTF-8">
    <title>Document</title>
    <link rel="stylesheet" type="text/css" href="main.css">
    <script src="./node_modules/web3/dist/web3.min.js">
    </script>
</head>
<body>
    <div class="container">
        <h1>Ethereum Betting</h1>
        <center>
            <label for="numberToWager"
                class="col-lg-2 control-label">
                Number to wager
            </label>
            <input id="numberToWager" type="text">
            <label for="etherToWager"
                class="col-lg-2 control-label">
                Number of ethers to wager
            </label>
            <input id="etherToWager" type="text">
            <button id="btnBet">Bet</button>
            <hr/>
            <h2 id="result"></h2>
            <h2 id="status"></h2>
        </center>
    </div>
```

```
<script src="https://code.jquery.com/jquery-3.2.1.slim.min.js">
</script>
<script>
    if (typeof web3 !== 'undefined') {
        // this statement is executed if you are using
        // MetaMask
        async function enableAccounts() {
            await ethereum.enable();
        }
        enableAccounts();
    } else {
        // set the provider you want from Web3.providers
        web3 = new Web3(
            new Web3.providers.HttpProvider(
            "http://localhost:8545"));
    }

    var abi = [ { "constant": false, "inputs": [], "name": "kill",
    "outputs": [], "payable": false, "stateMutability": "nonpayable",
    "type": "function" }, { "constant": true, "inputs": [], "name":
    "getStatus", "outputs": [ { "name": "", "type": "uint256" },
    { "name": "", "type": "uint256" } ], "payable": false,
    "stateMutability": "view", "type": "function" }, { "constant":
    false, "inputs": [ { "name": "number", "type": "uint256" } ],
    "name": "bet", "outputs": [], "payable": true, "stateMutability":
    "payable", "type": "function" }, { "constant": true, "inputs": [],
    "name": "getWinningNumber", "outputs": [ { "name": "", "type":
    "uint256" } ], "payable": false, "stateMutability": "view",
    "type": "function" }, { "inputs": [ { "name": "_minWager", "type":
    "uint256" } ], "payable": false, "stateMutability": "nonpayable",
    "type": "constructor" }, { "anonymous": false, "inputs": [ {
    "indexed": false, "name": "number", "type": "uint256" } ], "name":
    "WinningNumber", "type": "event" }, { "anonymous": false, "inputs":
    [ { "indexed": false, "name": "players", "type": "uint256" }, {
    "indexed": false, "name": "maxPlayers", "type": "uint256" } ],
    "name": "Status", "type": "event" } ]
```

```
var bettingContract = web3.eth.contract(abi)

//---change the address below to that of your own---
var contractAddress =
    '0x5491ecc1c403315cddd402b57990a3c5c6c50c63';
var contract = bettingContract.at(contractAddress);

var _minWager = 1;

//---event---
var winningNumberEvent = contract.WinningNumber();
winningNumberEvent.watch((error, result) => {
    if (!error){
        $("#result").html("Winning Number is: " +
            result.args.number);
    }
});

//---event---
var statusEvent = contract.Status();
statusEvent.watch((error, result) => {
    if (!error){
        $("#status").html("Status: " +
            result.args.players +
            " of " + result.args.maxPlayers);
    }
});

//---get the status of the game---
contract.getStatus(
    (error, result) => {
        if (!error){
            $("#status").html("Status: " +
                result[0].c[0] +
                " of " + result[1].c[0]);
        }
});
```

```
        $("#btnBet").click(function() {
            var numberToWager = $("#numberToWager").val();
            var etherToWager = $("#etherToWager").val();
            contract.bet(numberToWager, {
                gas: 300000,
                from: web3.eth.defaultAccount,
                value: web3.toWei(etherToWager, 'ether')
            }, (err, result) => {
                if (err){
                    $("#result").html(err);
                } else {
                    $("#result").html(
                    "Number has been submitted for betting.");
                }
            });
        });
    </script>
</body>
</html>
```

To test the web front end, type the following commands in Terminal:

```
$ cd ~/webprojects
$ serve
```

Using two instances of the Chrome browser, load each browser with the following URL: http://localhost:5000/OnlineBetting.html. You should see both display the same status (see Figure 10-19).

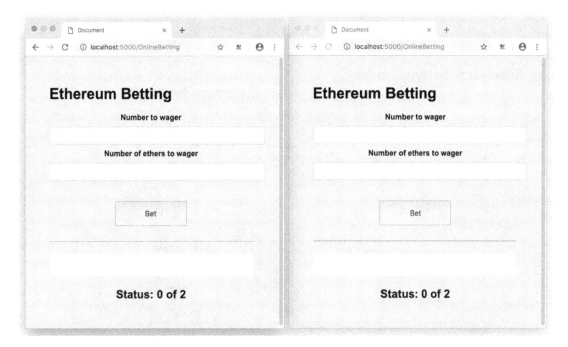

Figure 10-19. *Two instances of Chrome displaying the same page and game status*

Using Account 1, on the left browser, place a bet on the number 1 using 2 Ethers, and click the **Bet** button. Observe that MetaMask will pop up a window showing the amount to be sent to the contract. Click **CONFIRM**. Once you click the CONFIRM button, the first browser will show the message "*Number has been submitted for betting*" (see Figure 10-20).

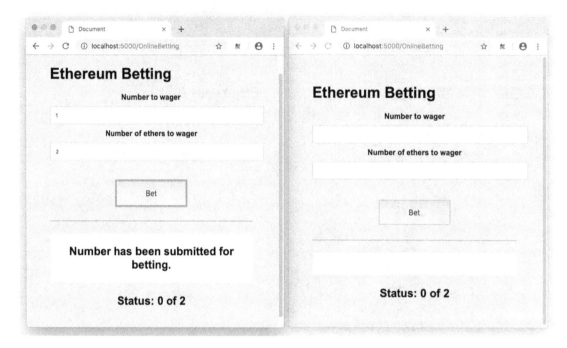

Figure 10-20. *The browser on the left has just betted on a number*

When the transaction has been confirmed, both browsers will update the status of the game (see Figure 10-21).

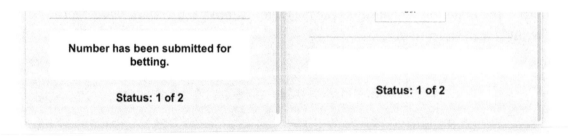

Figure 10-21. *Both browsers now show the updated status of the game*

Now switch to Account 2 on the second web browser and bet on the number 3 with 1 Ether. Click **Confirm** when the pop-up from MetaMask shows.

Once the transaction is confirmed, you should see the winning number and status of the game on both browsers (see Figure 10-22).

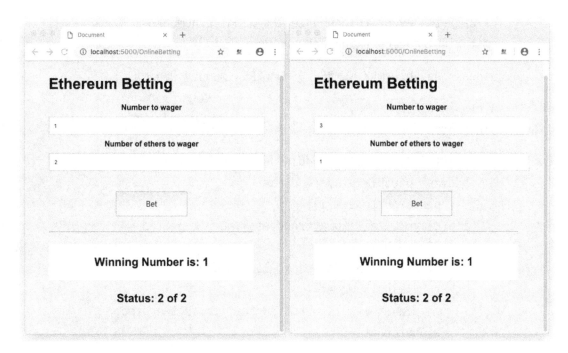

Figure 10-22. *Both browsers showing the winning number*

Returning Ethers Back to the Owner at the End of the Game

One issue we observed with the contract earlier in this chapter is that at the end of the game, we need to kill the contract in order to get back the Ethers held by the contract (when no one wins the game). Wouldn't it be better if you could transfer the remaining Ethers back to the owners automatically at the end of the game instead of having to kill it?

This is what we will do in this section. Make the following additions to the contract in the Remix IDE:

```
function announceWinners() private {
    //winningNumber =
    //uint(keccak256(abi.encodePacked(block.timestamp))) %
    //  MAX_WINNING_NUMBER + 1;

    // hard code the winning number to see what happens
    // when the contract is killed
    winningNumber = 1;
```

```
// call the event to announce the winning number
emit WinningNumber(winningNumber);

address payable[MAX_NUMBER_OF_WAGERS] memory winners ;

uint winnerCount = 0;
uint totalWinningWager = 0;

for (uint i=0; i < playerAddresses.length; i++) {
    address payable playerAddress =
        playerAddresses[i];
    if (playerDetails[playerAddress].numberWagered ==
        winningNumber) {
        winners[winnerCount] = playerAddress;
        totalWinningWager +=
            playerDetails[playerAddress].amountWagered;
        winnerCount++;
    }
}

for (uint j=0; j<winnerCount; j++) {
    winners[j].transfer(
        (playerDetails[winners[j]].amountWagered /
        totalWinningWager) * totalWager);
}

// if there is no winner, transfer all
// the remaining ethers back to owner
if (winnerCount==0) {
    owner.transfer(address(this).balance);
}
```

To get the balance of Ethers held by the contract, you can use the balance property of an account. The address(this) statement returns the address of the current contract.

To test the modified contract, redeploy the contract using Account 1 and use Account 2 and 3 to play the game:

- Deploy the contract and update the contract address in the OnlineBetting.html file.

- Observe balance of Account 1.

- Reload the OnlineBetting.html page using the Chrome browser.

- Using Account 2, bet on number 2 using 1 Ether.

- Using Account 3, bet on number 3 using 1 Ether

When the winning number is announced (which is still a 1 since we have hardcoded the contract to return 1 as the winning number), check the balance of Account 1. It should have 2 additional Ethers, which is transferred by the contract since no one wins the game).

Making the Game Run Indefinitely

So far our game stops when two players have played. And in order to get back all the Ethers, you have to kill the contract. A much better option is to make the game run indefinitely. That is, after the winning number is drawn, the contract automatically pays out either to the players or the owner and the game starts all over again.

To do this, add the following statements in bold to the contract:

...

```
function bet(uint number) public payable {
    require(playerAddressesMapping[msg.sender] == false);
    require(number >=1 && number <= MAX_WINNING_NUMBER);
    require( (msg.value / (1 ether)) >= minWager);

    // record the number and amount wagered by the player
    playerDetails[msg.sender].amountWagered = msg.value;
    playerDetails[msg.sender].numberWagered = number;

    playerAddresses.push(msg.sender);
    playerAddressesMapping[msg.sender] = true;

    numberOfWagers++;
    totalWager += msg.value;

    if (numberOfWagers >= MAX_NUMBER_OF_WAGERS) {
        announceWinners();
```

```
        //---start a new game---
        // remove all the player addresses mappings
        removeAllPlayersFromMapping();

        // remove all the addresses in the array
        delete playerAddresses;

        // reset the variables
        totalWager = 0;
        numberOfWagers = 0;
        winningNumber = 999;
    }
    emit Status(numberOfWagers, MAX_NUMBER_OF_WAGERS);
}

function removeAllPlayersFromMapping() private {
    for (uint i=0; i < playerAddresses.length; i++) {
        delete playerAddressesMapping[playerAddresses[i]];
    }
}
...
```

To start a new game, you remove all the players' address and reset the necessary variables. When you now redeploy the contract, the game can be played indefinitely.

Summary

In this chapter, you learned how to build an online lottery game. Apart from using the knowledge that you have learned from the previous few chapters, you have learned quite a number of new things, such as:

- How to get the Ethers held by a contract to refund to the owner by killing it

- How to transfer Ethers programmatically to another account

- How to use Etherscan to view the internal transfers made in a contract

In the next chapter, you will learn about tokens and how you can use them in your Smart Contracts.

## CHAPTER 11

Creating Your Tokens

If you have been following the previous chapters, you should now have a pretty good understanding of Ethereum Smart Contracts and how to interact with them through the web3.js APIs.

One exciting feature of Ethereum Smart Contracts is Ethereum tokens. Tokens are digital assets built on top of the Ethereum blockchain. Using tokens, developers can use it to pay for services performed by Smart Contracts, as well as use it as a mean for fund raising. Tokens also drive demands for Ether, the native cryptocurrency on the Ethereum blockchain.

In this chapter, you will learn what tokens are, how they are created, how to buy them, and how to add them to your MetaMask accounts.

What Are Tokens?

To understand the concept of tokens, let's start off with a real-life analogy. Most people are familiar with carnival (or fun fair). To play the games at the carnival, the stalls usually do not accept cash payment. Instead, they need you to exchange your cash (or use credit card) to purchase coins (or commonly called tokens) so that you can use them at the game stalls (see Figure 11-1).

Figure 11-1. *Tokens used in the real world at carnival games*

© Wei-Meng Lee 2019
W.-M. Lee, *Beginning Ethereum Smart Contracts Programming*,
https://doi.org/10.1007/978-1-4842-5086-0_11

The owner of the carnival do this for a variety of reasons:

- The stalls need not deal with cash; this will prevent the owner of the stalls (usually employees of the carnival owner) from pocketing the cash.

- The owner of the carnival receives cash up front before you even play the games; and all unused tokens cannot be refunded.

- The owner of the carnival wants to sell you more tokens than you need by giving you incentives to buy more up front.

In the cryptocurrency world, the same concepts apply to tokens. Instead of using fiat currency to buy the tokens directly, you first buy your Ethers, and then use Ethers to buy the tokens (see Figure 11-2).

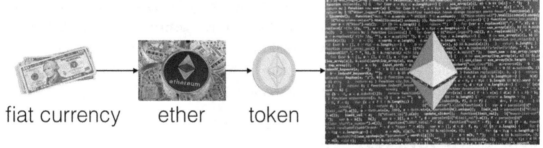

token to be used on your smart contract running on the Ethereum network

Figure 11-2. *Tokens on the Ethereum blockchain*

COINS VS. TOKENS

In the cryptocurrency world, there has been two terms that have been used interchangeably – **coins** and **tokens**. So are they the same? First, the definition of a *coin* is that it is an asset that is native to its own blockchain. Examples of coins are Bitcoin, Litecoin, and Ether. Each of these coins exists on their own blockchain. *Tokens*, on the other hand, are created on existing blockchains. The most common token platform is Ethereum, which allows developers to create their own tokens using the ERC20 standard (more on this in the later section of this chapter). Using Ether (which is the coin native to the Ethereum blockchain), users can exchange them for specific tokens on the Ethereum blockchain.

Hence, strictly speaking, coins are not the same as tokens. In fact, tokens are based on coins.

How Tokens Are Implemented?

Now that you have a clear understanding of tokens and how they work, let's see how tokens are implemented in Ethereum.

Tokens are implemented using Smart Contracts (yes, the same Smart Contracts that you have read in the previous few chapters) known as *token contracts*. A token contract is a Smart Contract that contains a mapping of account addresses and their balances. Figure 11-3 shows an example of the mapping.

Account Addresses	Balance
0x0000...0000	0
0x1234...9a7c	80
0x2a45...9c12	20
0x3d4f...7e2a	100

Total Tokens: **200**

Figure 11-3. *Token contract contains a map of account addresses and their balances*

Minting New Tokens

The total supply of tokens can be increased by *minting* new tokens. That is, you (the owner of the token contract) simply increase the balance of an account as shown in Figure 11-4.

Account Addresses	Balance
0x0000...0000	0
0x1234...9a7c	80
0x2a45...9c12	20
0x3d4f...7e2a	**200**

Total Tokens: ***300***

Figure 11-4. *Minting new tokens by increasing the balance of one or more accounts*

Burning Tokens

The total supply of tokens can be decreased by burning tokens. That is, you reduce the amount of balance of an account, as shown in Figure 11-5.

Account Addresses	Balance
0x0000…0000	0
0x1234…9a7c	~~80~~ 50
0x2a45…9c12	20
0x3d4f…7e2a	200

Total Tokens: **270**

***Figure 11-5.** Burning tokens by decreasing the balance of an account*

Tokens can also be burned by sending them to a dead address, as shown in Figure 11-6. Note that in this case the total supply of tokens does not change.

Account Addresses	Balance
0x0000…0000	**10**
0x1234…9a7c	50
0x2a45…9c12	20
0x3d4f…7e2a	~~200~~ 190

Total Tokens: **270**

***Figure 11-6.** Burning tokens by sending tokens to a dead address; in this case the total supply does not change*

Units Used Internally in Token Contracts

In token contracts, *decimal places of precision* represent how divisible a token can be. For example, consider the example of a fictitious token – **MusicToken**, with each token representing the right to own a song. In this case, the *decimal places of precision* would be set to 0. This means that the tokens cannot have a fractional component – you cannot have 1.1 or 1.5 tokens. In other words, the number of MusicToken one can own must be a discrete number (only integer values). Figure 11-7 shows how MusicTokens are represented internally within the token contract.

Internal representation
Decimals: 0
MusicToken

Account Addresses	Balance
0x0000…0000	0
0x1234…9a7c	8
0x2a45…9c12	2
0x3d4f…7e2a	5

Total Tokens: **15**

***Figure 11-7.** Token with 0 decimal precision have no fractional component*

Consider another example, the fictitious **GoldToken**, which represents the amount of gold a person owns. In this case, the decimal places of precision could be set to 3, which means that the amount of GoldToken a person owns can be down to 3 decimal places, such as 2.003. Figure 11-8 shows an example of how the balance of the GoldToken is represented internally and how the view to the user looks like.

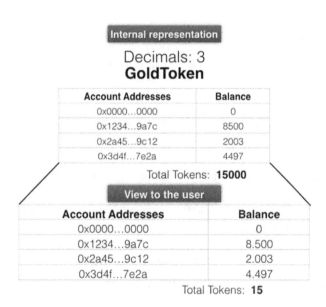

Figure 11-8. *Token with three decimal precisions, stored internally and viewed from outside*

Internally, for a token with n-decimals of precision, the balance is represented using this formula: ***token_internal = token_external * 10n***

For example, a user may own 4.497 GoldToken, but internally, the token contract stores its balance as 4497.

ERC20 Token Standard

In order for tokens created on the Ethereum blockchain to be accepted by Smart Contracts, tokens must adhere to some particular standards. In the case of Ethereum tokens, that standard is ERC20. ERC stands for *Ethereum Request for Comments*. In ERC20, the number 20 refers to the proposal ID number. The proposal ERC20 defines a set of rules which need to be met for a token to be able to interact with each other.

Tip   ERC20 standard is a specific set of functions developers must use in their tokens.

ERC20 tokens must be able to

- Get the total token supply

- Get the account balance

- Transfer the token from one account to another

- Approve the use of token as a monetary asset

Specifically, ERC20 tokens must implement the following interface:

```
contract ERC20Interface {
    function totalSupply() public constant returns (uint);

    function balanceOf(address tokenOwner) public constant
        returns (uint balance);

    function allowance(address tokenOwner, address
        spender) public constant returns (uint remaining);

    function transfer(address to, uint tokens) public
        returns (bool success);

    function approve(address spender, uint tokens) public
        returns (bool success);

    function transferFrom(address from, address to, uint
        tokens) public returns (bool success);

    event Transfer(address indexed from, address indexed
        to, uint tokens);
    event Approval(address indexed tokenOwner, address
        indexed spender, uint tokens);
}
```

Here are the uses for the various functions and events in the ERC20Interface:

- totalSupply – Returns the total token supply.

- balanceOf(address _owner) – Returns the account balance of
  _owner.

- transfer(address _to, uint256 _value) – Transfers _value to _to
  and fire the Transfer event. The function should revert if the _from
  account does not have enough tokens to spend.

- approve(address _spender, uint256 _value) – Allows _spender to
  withdraw from the account several times, up to the _value amount.

- transferFrom(address _from, address _to, uint256 _value) –
  Transfers _value from _from to _to and fire the Transfer event. The
  function should revert unless the _from account has deliberately
  authorized the sender of the message via some mechanism.

- allowance(address _owner, address _spender) – Returns the
  amount which the _spender is still allowed to withdraw from the
  _owner.

- Transfer(address indexed _from, address indexed _to,
  uint256 _value) – Must trigger when tokens are transferred,
  including zero-value transfers.

- Approval(address indexed _owner, address indexed _
  spender, uint256 _value) – Must trigger on any successful call to
  approve(address _spender, uint256 _value).

Creating Token Contracts

As mentioned in the earlier section, to create tokens, you need to create a token contract.
Fortunately, you can make use of some standard token contract that is already written
for you. For our example, we are going to write our token contract

based on the contract by **Token-Factory** (https://github.com/ConsenSys/Token-
Factory/tree/master/contracts).

Paste the following token contract into the Remix IDE:

Tip   You will be able to download the following token contract from the Apress support web site for this book.

```
pragma solidity ^0.4;

contract Token {

    /// @return total amount of tokens
    function totalSupply() constant returns
        (uint256 supply) {}

    /// @param _owner The address from which the balance will
    /// be retrieved
    /// @return The balance
    function balanceOf(address _owner) constant returns
        (uint256 balance) {}

    /// @notice send `_value` token to `_to` from `msg.sender`
    /// @param _to The address of the recipient
    /// @param _value The amount of token to be transferred
    /// @return Whether the transfer was successful or not
    function transfer(address _to, uint256 _value) returns
        (bool success) {}

    /// @notice send `_value` token to `_to` from `_from` on
    /// the condition
    /// it is approved by `_from`
    /// @param _from The address of the sender
    /// @param _to The address of the recipient
    /// @param _value The amount of token to be transferred
    /// @return Whether the transfer was successful or not
    function transferFrom(address _from, address _to,
        uint256 _value)
        returns (bool success) {}

    /// @notice `msg.sender` approves `_addr` to spend
    /// `_value` tokens
```

```
/// @param _spender The address of the account able to
/// transfer the tokens
/// @param _value The amount of wei to be approved for
/// transfer
/// @return Whether the approval was successful or not
function approve(address _spender, uint256 _value)
    returns (bool success) {}

/// @param _owner The address of the account owning tokens
/// @param _spender The address of the account able to
/// transfer the tokens
/// @return Amount of remaining tokens allowed to spent
function allowance(address _owner, address _spender)
    constant returns (uint256 remaining) {}

event Transfer(address indexed _from, address indexed _to,
            uint256 _value);

event Approval(address indexed _owner,
    address indexed _spender, uint256 _value);
}

/*
This implements ONLY the standard functions and NOTHING else.
For a token like you would want to deploy in something like Mist, see
HumanStandardToken.sol.

If you deploy this, you won't have anything useful.

Implements ERC 20 Token standard: https://github.com/ethereum/EIPs/issues/20
.
*/

contract StandardToken is Token {

    function transfer(address _to, uint256 _value) returns
        (bool success) {
        //Default assumes totalSupply can't be over
        /// max (2^256 - 1).
```

```
        //If your token leaves out totalSupply and can issue
        /// more tokens as
        // time goes on, you need to check if it doesn't wrap.
        //Replace the if with this one instead.
        //if (balances[msg.sender] >= _value && balances[_to]
        /// + _value >
        // balances[_to]) {
        if (balances[msg.sender] >= _value && _value > 0) {
            balances[msg.sender] -= _value;
            balances[_to] += _value;
            Transfer(msg.sender, _to, _value);
            return true;
        } else { return false; }
    }

    function transferFrom(address _from, address _to,
        uint256 _value)
        returns (bool success) {
        //same as above. Replace this line with the following
        // if you want to protect against wrapping uints.
        //if (balances[_from] >= _value &&
        // allowed[_from][msg.sender] >=
        // _value && balances[_to] + _value > balances[_to]) {
        if (balances[_from] >= _value &&
        allowed[_from][msg.sender] >= _value && _value > 0) {
            balances[_to] += _value;
            balances[_from] -= _value;
            allowed[_from][msg.sender] -= _value;
            Transfer(_from, _to, _value);
            return true;
        } else { return false; }
    }

    function balanceOf(address _owner) constant returns
        (uint256 balance) {
        return balances[_owner];
    }
```

```
    function approve(address _spender, uint256 _value)
    returns (bool success) {
        allowed[msg.sender][_spender] = _value;
        Approval(msg.sender, _spender, _value);
        return true;
    }

    function allowance(address _owner, address _spender)
        constant returns (uint256 remaining) {
      return allowed[_owner][_spender];
    }

    mapping (address => uint256) balances;
    mapping (address => mapping (address => uint256)) allowed;
    uint256 public totalSupply;
}

/*
This Token Contract implements the standard token functionality (https://
github.com/ethereum/EIPs/issues/20) as well as the following OPTIONAL
extras intended for use by humans.

In other words. This is intended for deployment in something like a Token
Factory or Mist wallet, and then used by humans.
Imagine coins, currencies, shares, voting weight, and so on.
Machine-based, rapid creation of many tokens would not necessarily need
these extra features or will be minted in other manners.

1) Initial Finite Supply (upon creation one specifies how much is minted).
2) In the absence of a token registry: Optional Decimal, Symbol & Name.
3) Optional approveAndCall() functionality to notify a contract if an
   approval() has occurred.

.
*/

contract MyToken is StandardToken {

    /* Public variables of the token */

    /*
```

```
NOTE:
The following variables are OPTIONAL vanities. One
does not have to include them.
They allow one to customise the token contract & in
no way influences the core functionality.
Some wallets/interfaces might not even bother to look
at this information.
*/
string public name;        // fancy name: eg Simon Bucks
uint8 public decimals;     // How many decimals to show. ie.
                           // There could 1000 base units
                           // with 3 decimals. Meaning 0.980
                           // SBX = 980 base units. It's
                           // like comparing 1 wei to 1
                           // ether.
string public symbol;      // An identifier: eg SBX
string public version = 'H0.1';   // human 0.1 standard.
                                  // Just an arbitrary
                                  // versioning scheme.

function MyToken(
    uint256 _initialAmount,
    string _tokenName,
    uint8 _decimalUnits,
    string _tokenSymbol
    ) {
    balances[msg.sender] = _initialAmount;
        // Give the creator all initial tokens
    totalSupply = _initialAmount;   // Update total supply
    name = _tokenName;              // Set the name for
                                    // display purposes
    decimals = _decimalUnits;       // Amount of decimals
                                    // for display
                                    // purposes
    symbol = _tokenSymbol;    // Set the symbol for display
```

```
                             // purposes
}

/* Approves and then calls the receiving contract */
function approveAndCall(address _spender, uint256 _value,
    bytes _extraData) returns (bool success) {
    allowed[msg.sender][_spender] = _value;
    Approval(msg.sender, _spender, _value);

    // call the receiveApproval function on the contract
    // you want to be notified. This crafts the function
    // signature manually so one doesn't have to include
    // a contract in here just for this.
    //receiveApproval(address _from, uint256 _value,
    // address
    // _tokenContract, bytes _extraData)
    //it is assumed that when does this that the call
    // *should* succeed,
    // otherwise one would use vanilla approve instead.
    if(!_spender.call(bytes4(bytes32(sha3(
      "receiveApproval(address,uint256, address,bytes)"))),
      msg.sender, _value, this, _extraData)) { throw; }
    return true;
  }
}
```

Caution   For this contract, you need to use the older 0.4 Solidity compiler.

Based on the token contract (MyToken), we will customize it by adding the following statements in bold:

```
contract MyToken is StandardToken {

    /* Public variables of the token */

    /*
```

```
NOTE:
The following variables are OPTIONAL vanities. One
does not have to include them.
They allow one to customise the token contract & in
no way influences the core functionality.
Some wallets/interfaces might not even bother to look
at this information.
*/
string public name;        // fancy name: eg Simon Bucks
uint8 public decimals;     // How many decimals to show. ie.
                           // There could 1000 base units
                           // with 3 decimals. Meaning 0.980
                           // SBX = 980 base units. It's
                           // like comparing 1 wei to 1
                           // ether.
string public symbol;      // An identifier: eg SBX
string public version = 'H0.1';   // human 0.1 standard.
                                  // Just an arbitrary
                                  // versioning scheme.

// how many tokens per 1 ETH
uint256 public unitsOneEthCanBuy;

// total amount raised in WEI
uint256 public totalEthInWei;

// the owner of the raised ETH
address public fundsWallet;

function MyToken(
    uint256 _initialAmount,
    string _tokenName,
    uint8 _decimalUnits,
    string _tokenSymbol
    ) {
    balances[msg.sender] = _initialAmount;
        // Give the creator all initial tokens
```

```
    totalSupply = _initialAmount;   // Update total supply
    name = _tokenName;              // Set the name for
                                    // display purposes
    decimals = _decimalUnits;       // Amount of decimals
                                    // for display
                                    // purposes
    symbol = _tokenSymbol;     // Set the symbol for display
                               // purposes

    // 10 tokens for 1 ETH
    unitsOneEthCanBuy = 10;

    // owner of the contract gets ETH
    fundsWallet = msg.sender;
}

/* Approves and then calls the receiving contract */
function approveAndCall(address _spender, uint256 _value,
    bytes _extraData) returns (bool success) {
    allowed[msg.sender][_spender] = _value;
    Approval(msg.sender, _spender, _value);
    ...
}

function() payable{
    // msg.value is in Wei
    totalEthInWei = totalEthInWei + msg.value;

    // amount is the token bought by the sender
    uint256 amount = msg.value * unitsOneEthCanBuy;

    // balances stores the tokens held by the
    // various parties
    if (balances[fundsWallet] < amount) {
        return;
    }

    balances[fundsWallet] =
        balances[fundsWallet] - amount;
```

271

```
    balances[msg.sender]  =
        balances[msg.sender]  + amount;

    // Transfer is an event
    Transfer(fundsWallet, msg.sender, amount);
    // Broadcast a message to the blockchain

    // transfer ether to fundsWallet
    fundsWallet.transfer(msg.value);
    }
}
```

The preceding statements specify the price of the token (10 tokens for 1 Ether). It also specifies that the raised ETH would go to the owner (the one who published the contract).

The payable() function is called when Ether is sent to the contract. It converts the Ether sent to tokens and credit the tokens to the respective buyers. It also sends the Ether sent to the contract to the owner of the contract.

The total amount of tokens to be issued, as well as the token name, decimal places, and symbol will be set through the constructor of the token contract when the contract is deployed:

```
function MyToken(
    uint256 _initialAmount,
    string _tokenName,
    uint8 _decimalUnits,
    string _tokenSymbol
    ) {
```

Deploying the Token Contract

In the Remix IDE, under the **Compile** tab, select version **0.4.26** of the Solidity compiler (see Figure 11-9).

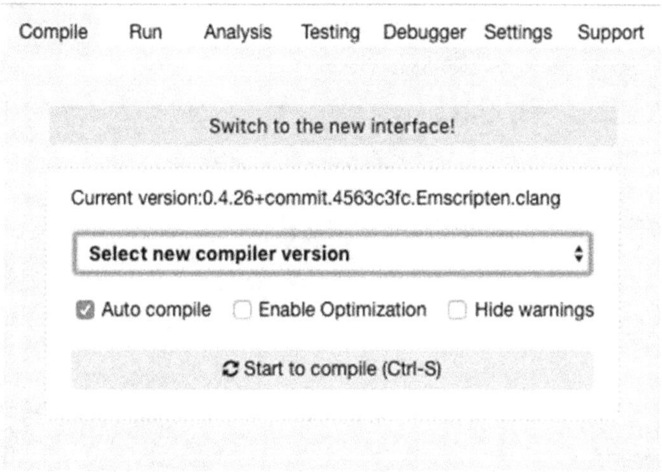

Figure 11-9. *Compile the token contract with 0.4.26 version of the compiler*

For this example, you will issue the following:

- A total of 2000 tokens

- 18 decimal places of precision

- Token Name of "**Lee Token**"

- Token symbol of "**LWM**"

Based on these values, the initial amount for this token would be 2000 x 10^{18}, or 2,000,000,000,000,000,000,000 (2 followed by 21 zeros). Hence the constructor for the contract would be

```
"2000000000000000000000", "Lee Token", 18, "LWM"
```

Type the preceding constructor into the Remix IDE and click the **Deploy** button (see Figure 11-10). Click **CONFIRM** to submit the transaction.

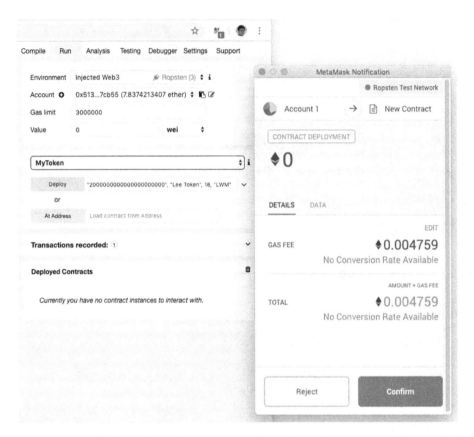

Figure 11-10. *Deploying the token contract based on the 2000 tokens and 18 decimal places of precision*

Once the contract is successfully deployed, record its contract address (see Figure 11-11).

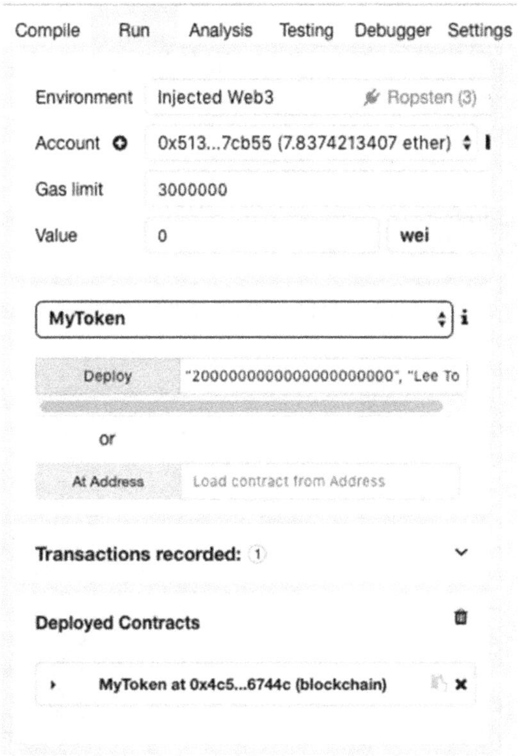

Figure 11-11. *Take note of the token contract address after it has been successfully deployed*

For my example, the address of my token contract is 0x4c5167a4df68f05722d0afdf 57d734a575d6744c.

Adding Tokens to MetaMask

Once the token contract is deployed, you can add it to MetaMask. In MetaMask, click the **Menu** icon (see Figure 11-12).

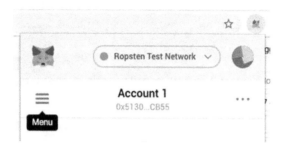

Figure 11-12. *Click the Menu on MetaMask so that you can add a token to your account*

Click **Add Token** (see Figure 11-13).

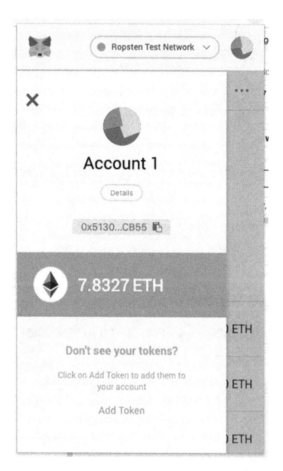

Figure 11-13. *Click the Add Token link to add a token to your account*

Click the **Custom Token** tab and paste the token contract address that you have copied previously into the **Token Contract Address** field. Once you have pasted in the token contract address, the token symbol and decimals of precision would be populated automatically. Click **Next** (see Figure 11-14).

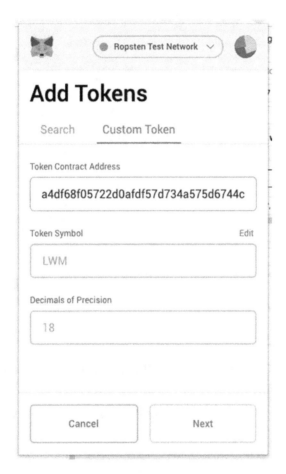

Figure 11-14. *Specifying the address of the token contract and the symbol and decimals of precision of the token will automatically appear*

You should now see the token as shown in Figure 11-15. Click **Add Tokens**.

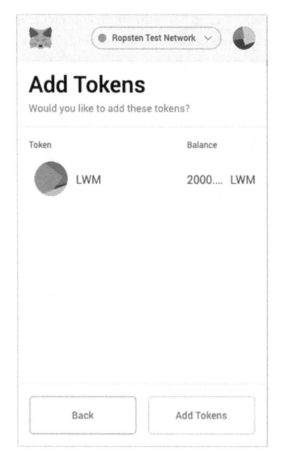

Figure 11-15. *Click Add Tokens to add the token to your account*

The token is now added to your account (see Figure 11-16).

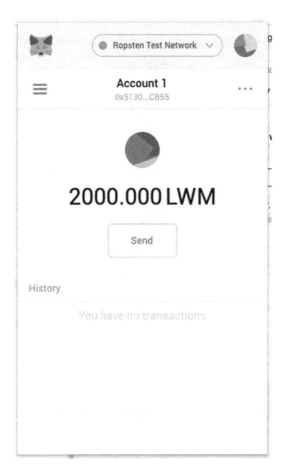

Figure 11-16. *The token added to your account*

Buying Tokens

When the token contract is deployed, all the initial tokens would belong to the account that deployed the token contract (which is Account 1 in this example). If a user wants to buy tokens, all he needs to do is to send some Ethers to the token contract, and the token contract will automatically transfer some tokens to his account (all balances are maintained by the token contract). For this example, we shall get a user (Account 2) to buy some tokens.

Before you buy any tokens, take note of the balance of Account 1 (which you have used to deploy the token contract). For my own record, my Account 1 at this moment has 7.8327 Ethers.

Tip   When Account 2 sends some Ether to the token contract, the Ethers will be credited into Account 1 (who owns the tokens).

In MetaMask, switch to Account 2 (see Figure 11-17). Then, click **Send**:

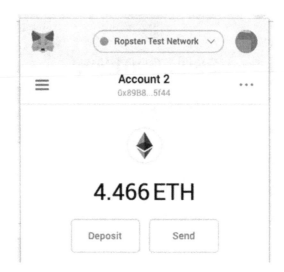

Figure 11-17. *Click Send to send some Ethers to the token contract in exchange for some tokens*

Enter the token contract address that you have copied earlier and enter 1 for the amount of Ether to send to the contract (see Figure 11-18). Click **Next** and then **Confirm** to send the transaction.

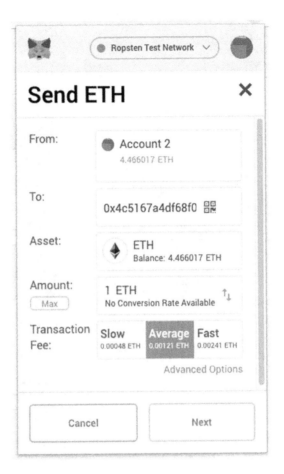

Figure 11-18. *Sending 1 Ether to the token contract*

Once the transaction is confirmed, click the Menu icon and click **Add Token** (see Figure 11-19).

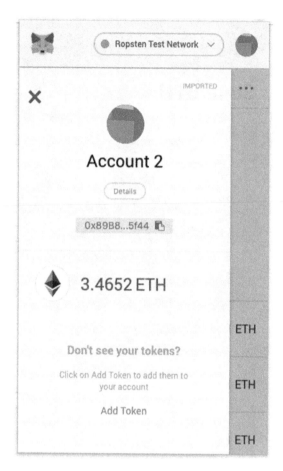

Figure 11-19. *Adding a token to Account 2*

Enter the address of the token contract and click **Next**. You should now see the Account 2 has 10 LWM tokens (see Figure 11-20). Click **Add Tokens**.

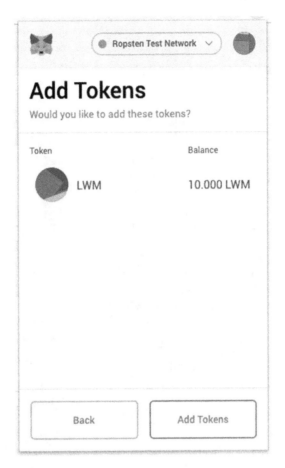

Figure 11-20. *Sending 1 Ether to the token contract gives the account 10 LWM tokens*

In MetaMask, switch to Account 1 (see Figure 11-21). Observe that Account 1 is now 1 Ether richer and the token balance is now 1990 LWM (10 tokens has been transferred to Account 2).

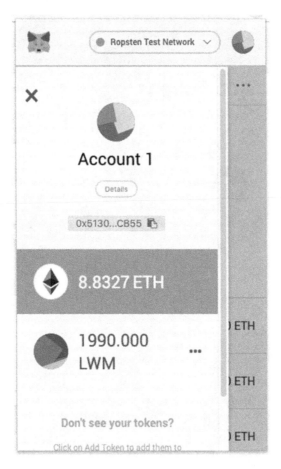

Figure 11-21. *Account 1 is now 1 Ether richer but 10 LWM tokens poorer*

Creating an ICO Page

Now that you have created a token, it is time to spread the word and get people to buy it. In the cryptocurrency world, an **Initial Coin Offering** (ICO) is a fundraising event that allows companies to raise funds through the sale of their coins (or tokens).

The next thing you need to do is to see how much of the tokens have been sold. Create a text file named **ICO.html** and save it the ~/**web3projects** directory. Populate the **ICO.html** file as follows:

```
<!doctype html>
<html lang="en">
  <body>
    <center>
```

```
    <h1>LWM Coin ICO</h1>
    <h2>Total Amount Raised</h2>
    <p id="amountRaised"></p>
</center>
<script>
    var abi =
    [ { "constant": false, "inputs": [ { "name": "_spender", "type":
    "address" }, { "name": "_value", "type": "uint256" } ], "name":
    "approve", "outputs": [ { "name": "success", "type": "bool" } ],
    "payable": false, "stateMutability": "nonpayable", "type": "function"
    }, { "constant": false, "inputs": [ { "name": "_spender", "type":
    "address" }, { "name": "_value", "type": "uint256" }, { "name": "_
    extraData", "type": "bytes" } ], "name": "approveAndCall", "outputs":
    [ { "name": "success", "type": "bool" } ], "payable": false,
    "stateMutability": "nonpayable", "type": "function" }, { "constant":
    false, "inputs": [ { "name": "_to", "type": "address" }, { "name":
    "_value", "type": "uint256" } ], "name": "transfer", "outputs":
    [ { "name": "success", "type": "bool" } ], "payable": false,
    "stateMutability": "nonpayable", "type": "function" }, { "constant":
    false, "inputs": [ { "name": "_from", "type": "address" }, { "name":
    "_to", "type": "address" }, { "name": "_value", "type": "uint256" }
    ], "name": "transferFrom", "outputs": [ { "name": "success", "type":
    "bool" } ], "payable": false, "stateMutability": "nonpayable",
    "type": "function" }, { "inputs": [ { "name": "_initialAmount",
    "type": "uint256" }, { "name": "_tokenName", "type": "string" }, {
    "name": "_decimalUnits", "type": "uint8" }, { "name": "_tokenSymbol",
    "type": "string" } ], "payable": false, "stateMutability":
    "nonpayable", "type": "constructor" }, { "payable": true,
    "stateMutability": "payable", "type": "fallback" }, { "anonymous":
    false, "inputs": [ { "indexed": true, "name": "_from", "type":
    "address" }, { "indexed": true, "name": "_to", "type": "address" },
    { "indexed": false, "name": "_value", "type": "uint256" } ], "name":
    "Transfer", "type": "event" }, { "anonymous": false, "inputs": [ {
    "indexed": true, "name": "_owner", "type": "address" }, { "indexed":
    true, "name": "_spender", "type": "address" }, { "indexed": false,
    "name": "_value", "type": "uint256" } ], "name": "Approval",
```

```
"type": "event" }, { "constant": true, "inputs": [ { "name": "_
owner", "type": "address" }, { "name": "_spender", "type": "address"
} ], "name": "allowance", "outputs": [ { "name": "remaining", "type":
"uint256" } ], "payable": false, "stateMutability": "view", "type":
"function" }, { "constant": true, "inputs": [ { "name": "_owner",
"type": "address" } ], "name": "balanceOf", "outputs": [ {
"name": "balance", "type": "uint256" } ], "payable": false,
"stateMutability": "view", "type": "function" }, { "constant": true,
"inputs": [], "name": "decimals", "outputs": [ { "name": "",
"type": "uint8" } ], "payable": false, "stateMutability": "view",
"type": "function" }, { "constant": true, "inputs": [], "name":
"fundsWallet", "outputs": [ { "name": "", "type": "address" } ],
"payable": false, "stateMutability": "view", "type": "function" },
{ "constant": true, "inputs": [], "name": "name", "outputs":
[ { "name": "", "type": "string" } ], "payable": false,
"stateMutability": "view", "type": "function" }, { "constant":
true, "inputs": [], "name": "symbol", "outputs": [ { "name": "",
"type": "string" } ], "payable": false, "stateMutability": "view",
"type": "function" }, { "constant": true, "inputs": [], "name":
"totalEthInWei", "outputs": [ { "name": "", "type": "uint256" } ],
"payable": false, "stateMutability": "view", "type": "function" },
{ "constant": true, "inputs": [], "name": "totalSupply",
"outputs": [ { "name": "", "type": "uint256" } ], "payable": false,
"stateMutability": "view", "type": "function" }, { "constant": true,
"inputs": [], "name": "unitsOneEthCanBuy", "outputs": [ { "name": "",
"type": "uint256" } ], "payable": false, "stateMutability": "view",
"type": "function" }, { "constant": true, "inputs": [], "name":
"version", "outputs": [ { "name": "", "type": "string" } ],
"payable": false, "stateMutability": "view", "type": "function" } ]
  var MyContract = web3.eth.contract(abi);
  var myContractInstance = MyContract.at(
     '0x4c5167a4df68f05722d0afdf57d734a575d6744c');
  myContractInstance.totalEthInWei(function(err,data){
   document.getElementById('amountRaised').innerHTML =
    (data.toString(10)/1000000000000000000) + ' ETH';
  });
```

```
    </script>
  </body>
</html>
```

Tip   Be sure to replace the token contract address with that of your own. The **abi** variable contains the ABI of the **MyToken** contract.

In **Terminal**, type the following commands:

```
$ cd ~/web3projects
$ serve
```

Load the **ICO.html** page on the Chrome browser (with MetaMask connected to the Ropsten network) and you should see the amount raised by your token as shown in Figure 11-22.

Figure 11-22.   *The ICO.html page showing the amount raised by the LWM token*

Summary

In this chapter, you learned how tokens work and created one yourself using a token contract. You also learned how to add tokens to your MetaMask account and how you can buy tokens by sending Ethers to the token contract. Finally, you also learned how to display a page showing how much a token has sold.

287

Index

© Wei-Meng Lee 2019
W.-M. Lee, *Beginning Ethereum Smart Contracts Programming*,
https://doi.org/10.1007/978-1-4842-5086-0

CPSIA information can be obtained
at www.ICGtesting.com
Printed in the USA
LVHW101723110919
630731LV00004B/5/P

9 781484 250853